Unveiling NIST Cybersecurity Framework 2.0

Secure your organization with the practical applications of CSF

Jason Brown

Unveiling NIST Cybersecurity Framework 2.0

Group Product Manager: Dhruv J. Kataria

Publishing Product Manager: Neha Sharma

Book Project Manager: Uma Devi Lakshmikanth

Senior Editor: Sujata Tripathi

Technical Editor: Nithik Cheruvakodan

Copy Editor: Safis Editing

Proofreader: Sujata Tripathi

Indexer: Subalakshmi Govindhan

Production Designer: Gokul Raj S.T

DevRel Marketing Coordinator: Marylou D'mello

Business Development Executive: Shruthi Shetty

First published: December 2024

Production reference:1180924

Published by Packt Publishing Ltd.

Grosvenor House

11 St Paul's Square

Birmingham

B3 1RB, UK

ISBN 978-1-83546-307-9

www.packtpub.com

To my wife and daughter – words cannot express the love I have for both of you. I am so thankful to have you in my life. I love you both very much.

– Jason Brown

Contributors

About the author

Jason Brown's passions are data privacy, cybersecurity, and continuing education. Brown has spent his career working with small- to medium-sized businesses to large international organizations, developing robust privacy and cybersecurity programs. Brown has held titles such as chief information security officer, virtual chief information security officer, and data privacy officer.

Brown currently holds many industry-leading certifications, including ISC2's CISSP, ISACA's CDPSE and COBIT, and ITIL, and he also holds a bachelor of science degree from Central Michigan University and a master of science degree from Ferris State University.

I want to thank everyone for encouraging me to follow my dreams and allowing me to share my experiences with the world.

About the reviewers

Soufiane Adil is a distinguished information security and cybersecurity compliance expert, specializing in an extensive range of standards, including ISO 27001, ISO 31000, ISO 22301, PCI-DSS, ISO 42001, ISO 21434, NIST 800-171, CMMC, NIST 800-53, HIPAA, PIPEDA, SOC2, FedRamp, CIS, GDPR, and Law/Loi 25. With a proven track record of guiding enterprises through the complexities of cybersecurity frameworks, Soufiane ensures that organizations achieve and maintain rigorous compliance standards. His strategic approach not only addresses regulatory requirements but also enhances the overall security posture of organizations, making him a trusted advisor in the field of cybersecurity compliance.

Thomas Marsland is a cybersecurity leader with a focus on designing systems and processes that embrace security from the ground up while protecting scalability and minimizing technical debt. He enjoys working on problems in operations and technology, delivering value to organizations with a mission-focused mindset. A 22-year veteran of the United States Navy, his work history includes nuclear power, information technology, cybersecurity, and executive leadership in cybersecurity and information technology, including for the US Navy and as the VP of technology at Cloud Range. In his spare time, he leads VetSec, a 501c3 nonprofit with the mission to "create a world where no veteran pursuing a career goes unemployed."

Rajat Dubey, a cybersecurity expert with 13+ years of experience, safeguards global enterprises. His expertise is risk assessment, compliance, threat modeling, incident response, ethical hacking, digital forensics, cloud security, AI, blockchain, IoT, and quantum computing. He has an MEng in Cybersecurity Policy and Compliance from GWU, USA, and an MBA from Rotman UoT. He works with Fortune 500 clients across industries. He is a senior member of IEEE and a fellow of CSA. He publishes research papers, articles and peer-reviewed books. He is a trusted advisor, navigating complex challenges and developing innovative solutions.

Table of Contents

Part 2: NIST Cybersecurity Framework Functions

3

Govern   29

4

Identify   51

5

Protect   67

6

Detect   83

7

Respond   91

8

Recover   101

Part 3: Applying the Framework

9

How to Deal with Cyber Risk   111

10

Policies, Standards, and Procedures   125

11

Assessment   141

Preface

As cybersecurity continuously evolves, so too do your adversaries. The tactics and techniques they use today may not be the same that they use tomorrow. Would you know how to fend them off or respond to an incident if one were to occur? Frameworks are developed by industry experts to help you and your team align a cybersecurity program with a given standard.

This book will take you step by step through building out various aspects of your program. From identifying devices plugged into your network to establishing governance, and how to respond to an incident, a framework is meant to provide guidance for how to build these programs for your organization.

Who this book is for

This book is meant for those who are new to cybersecurity or who have never worked with the NIST Cybersecurity Framework before.

What this book covers

Chapter 1, Introduction to Cybersecurity Frameworks, will discuss what a framework is.

Chapter 2, NIST Cybersecurity Framework Fundamentals, will talk about the NIST Cybersecurity Framework and why you should use it.

Chapter 3, Govern, will review why governance is so important to a cybersecurity program.

Chapter 4, Identify, will highlight why you cannot protect what you cannot see, which is why identifying hardware and software is a key component of your program.

Chapter 5, Protect, will talk about protecting your environment and the sensitive data that resides in it, now that we have identified everything in our environment.

Chapter 6, Detect, will discuss how most IT resources generate logs for events. You must have a game plan for what you do with those logs and where they are placed.

Chapter 7, Respond, will teach how to respond to an incident when one occurs.

Chapter 8, Recover, will discuss best practices for recovering your IT resources after an incident has occurred.

Chapter 9, How to Deal with Cyber Risk, will explain how to reduce cyber risk throughout your organization.

Chapter 10, Policies, Standards, and Procedures, will talk about how policies need structure, help you to develop an easy-to-use method for creating policies, standards, and procedures, and discuss how they are arranged.

Chapter 11, Assessment, will give an overview of how to perform an assessment to better understand your current state, whether you are by yourself or you have a team of auditors.

To get the most out of this book

There are no technical requirements to get the most out of the book. You should have basic knowledge and understanding of IT and networking concepts.

Software/hardware covered in the book	Operating system requirements
Angular 9	Windows, macOS, or Linux
TypeScript 3.7	
ECMAScript 11	

Conventions used

There are a number of text conventions used throughout this book.

`Code in text`: Indicates code words in text, database table names, folder names, filenames, file extensions, pathnames, dummy URLs, user input, and Twitter handles. Here is an example: "If we were to change the contents of the file to, `This is a hashed file!`, the new results would be: `10b481d359a851de7efb58b1cc4f0b237014e37be60936ae22da52ac10eb7388`."

Bold: Indicates a new term, an important word, or words that you see onscreen. For instance, words in menus or dialog boxes appear in **bold**. Here is an example: "Even though you know you have to click the **Next** button 10 times to install a piece of software, state that."

> **Tips or important notes**
> Appear like this.

Get in touch

Feedback from our readers is always welcome.

General feedback: If you have questions about any aspect of this book, email us at `customercare@packtpub.com` and mention the book title in the subject of your message.

Errata: Although we have taken every care to ensure the accuracy of our content, mistakes do happen. If you have found a mistake in this book, we would be grateful if you would report this to us. Please visit www.packtpub.com/support/errata and fill in the form.

Piracy: If you come across any illegal copies of our works in any form on the internet, we would be grateful if you would provide us with the location address or website name. Please contact us at copyright@packt.com with a link to the material.

If you are interested in becoming an author: If there is a topic that you have expertise in and you are interested in either writing or contributing to a book, please visit authors.packtpub.com.

Share Your Thoughts

Once you've read *Unveiling NIST Cybersecurity Framework 2.0*, we'd love to hear your thoughts! Scan the QR code below to go straight to the Amazon review page for this book and share your feedback.

https://packt.link/r/183546307X

Your review is important to us and the tech community and will help us make sure we're delivering excellent quality content.

Download a free PDF copy of this book

Thanks for purchasing this book!

Do you like to read on the go but are unable to carry your print books everywhere?

Is your eBook purchase not compatible with the device of your choice?

Don't worry, now with every Packt book you get a DRM-free PDF version of that book at no cost.

Read anywhere, any place, on any device. Search, copy, and paste code from your favorite technical books directly into your application.

The perks don't stop there, you can get exclusive access to discounts, newsletters, and great free content in your inbox daily

Follow these simple steps to get the benefits:

1. Scan the QR code or visit the link below

https://packt.link/free-ebook/978-1-83546-307-9

2. Submit your proof of purchase

3. That's it! We'll send your free PDF and other benefits to your email directly

Part 1:
Why Select the NIST
Cybersecurity Framework?

To make progress in your cybersecurity journey, you need to align your program against a set of best practices. Frameworks are developed by industry leaders who come from different technological backgrounds. The NIST Cybersecurity Framework is no different. It was created by experts who work for the US federal government. In this section, we will discuss the reasons for its development and the need to align your program with it.

This part has the following chapters:

- *Chapter 1, Introduction to Cybersecurity Frameworks*
- *Chapter 2, NIST Cybersecurity Framework Fundamentals*

1

Introduction to Cybersecurity Frameworks

In this book, we take a deep dive into a framework developed by the **National Institute of Standards and Technology (NIST)** called the **Cybersecurity Framework (CSF)**. This framework was originally developed to better protect critical infrastructure businesses from threats, identify and handle **information technology (IT)** risks, and build resiliency into your IT and cybersecurity program.

In this chapter, we will take a look at the following topics:

- What is a framework?
- Why the NIST CSF?
- The history behind the NIST CSF
- Comparing the CSF to other frameworks
- NIST CSF success stories

What is a framework?

There are many ways to get a cybersecurity program off the ground, but where should you start? This can be intimidating to many IT professionals as cybersecurity has its own language. Frameworks are developed to assist organizations with this endeavor. A framework is used to align a program against best practices. It can also be a set of requirements that one must implement to perform a particular function.

Frameworks do not necessarily tell you how to implement a particular control, only that you should have it in place. For instance, a framework may state that you should implement **multi-factor authentication (MFA)**; however, it may not state how or where to implement it. The framework may state that you ensure proper auditing and logging is configured, but not state how to do it or how long you should keep the logs.

A framework is a document used to help the organization implement best practices. You, or the head of security, may decide that you do not intend to implement a control or a family of controls. That is perfectly fine; however, you must decide the level of risk you and the organization are willing to accept by not implementing a particular control or a control family. More on cybersecurity risk in *Chapter 9*.

Organizations such as the **International Organization for Standardization (ISO)** have produced frameworks to align organizations with cybersecurity best practices. ISO *27001/27002* are standards used by many international organizations to align themselves to cybersecurity best practices. Governments have also created cybersecurity standards used to protect them from adversaries who intend to do harm.

NIST is an agency within the US federal government. This agency has been directed to create several standards and frameworks, including frameworks used for cybersecurity. Australia has the **Australian Signals Directorate's Australian Cyber Security Centre (ASD's ACSC)**. Canada has the Centre for Cyber Security. Each of these government institutions has developed its own cybersecurity frameworks. There are also plenty of frameworks that align with regulatory requirements. While they too align with best practices, these are required frameworks that you must use. For example, the healthcare industry must abide by the **Health Insurance Portability and Accountability Act (HIPAA)**. If you take credit cards for payment purposes, then the **Payment Card Industry Data Security Standard (PCI DSS)** is the one for you. If you do not have to align with regulatory requirements, then there is no right or wrong framework to choose. However, you must first understand your business objectives and then choose a framework.

As you review which framework or frameworks you want to choose for your organization, you must understand the business objectives. This means that even though you chose a particular framework to implement, it could be quite possible that the business has requirements imposed on it. Those organizations are required to implement additional controls on top of what they already have in place.

For example, your organization has decided it wants to implement ISO *27001* as they are an international company. This is the baseline standard that has been chosen for your organization. The organization has decided that it also wants to process, store, and transmit credit card numbers as it sells products both in person and online. This also requires the organization to become compliant with PCI DSS) – yet another framework. The organization also conducts business in the **European Union (EU)**, which carries the requirement of the **General Data Protection Regulation (GDPR)**. GDPR dictates how organizations can process, store, and transmit highly sensitive **personally identifiable information (PII)**.

Maybe your organization performs work with the US federal government. According to the **Defense Federal Acquisition Regulation Supplement (DFARS)** *252.204-7012*, there are requirements that must be followed, which are set out in the **Special Publication (SP)** *800-171* framework. It may also require that any **Software-as-a-Service (SaaS)** application used as part of the government program be housed in a highly regulated environment such as the **Federal Risk and Authorization Management Program (FedRAMP)**.

You are now probably saying to yourself, "*This is great and all, but how does NIST fit into this picture?*"

Why not dive right in?

Why the NIST CSF?

The NIST CSF is a wonderful cybersecurity framework to start off with. It was meant for organizations that are considered critical infrastructure to assist in implementing cybersecurity controls. Also, it is free to consume. Well, it is not necessarily free – I mean if you are a US citizen, then your tax dollars paid for it to be developed.

Though it was originally written for critical infrastructure businesses, the NIST CSF 2.0 is meant to be easily adopted and used for small to medium-sized, even larger, organizations. The framework was written in such a way that it can be customizable when implemented. As you will see later on in this chapter, organizations that adopted other frameworks migrated to the CSF because they were hard to implement.

As mentioned, the CSF is a framework that is easy to understand, easy to maintain, and easy to score and show progress of how your cybersecurity program is maturing. It also sets you and your organization up for success if and when you decide to adopt another framework such as NIST's SP *800-53*, the **Center for Internet Security Critical Security Controls (CIS Controls)**, **Control Objectives for Information and Related Technologies (COBIT)**, and **ISO 27001**.

The NIST CSF 2.0 is broken down into six main core functions:

- Govern
- Identify
- Protect
- Detect
- Respond
- Recover

These six functions, explained in more detail in *Chapter 2*, are further broken down into categories and subcategories. The functions represent a common theme or family of controls used to protect the organization or build resiliency in the program. As an example, the Identify function has the following categories:

- Asset Management
- Risk Assessment
- Improvement

Each of these categories is further broken down into controls that should be implemented.

The history behind the NIST CSF

The 2000s and 2010s were a mess for IT and cybersecurity. Though the thought of implementing a cybersecurity program was far from people's minds, the concept started to grow. During the 2000s, we had viruses such as SQL Slammer, Code Red, Blaster, and Conficker, to name a few. These computer viruses wreaked havoc across many organizations, governments, and higher education institutions. When the 2010s came around, we had Stuxnet and Flame. However, in 2013, we began to see ransomware take hold with CryptoLocker.

Due to businesses being hit by malicious payloads, and many not knowing what to do or how to protect themselves, the Obama administration stepped in. In February 2013, the president signed Executive Order *13636*, named "*Improving Critical Infrastructure Cybersecurity*," directing NIST to develop a new framework for cybersecurity. In 2014, we saw the first edition of the CSF.

The early version of the CSF was aimed specifically toward those who owned and operated critical infrastructure. Though the framework was and is voluntary, these sectors are what the US considers critical to its operations:

- Agriculture
- Education
- Water
- Public health
- Transportation
- Electricity
- Security services
- Telecommunications
- Banking and finance

These are just a few of the types of organizations that are considered crucial under the critical infrastructure protection program.

Version 1.1 came out 4 years later with several improvements. A few of the improvements included the following:

- Clarification of controls and terms
- A new section on performing risk self-assessments
- Refined requirements around identity, credentialing, and access management

Version 2.0 was released in 2024. The new version kept the original five functions – Identify, Protect, Detect, Respond, and Recover. However, in version 2.0, a new function was introduced - Govern. Govern is meant to build in governance throughout the organization, governing builds in **enterprise risk management (ERM)**, along with an emphasis on cybersecurity supply chain risk management.

Comparing the CSF to other frameworks

As mentioned previously, there are several different cybersecurity frameworks to choose from. Each category and subcategory found in the NIST CSF aligns with other frameworks as well. There is an information reference that correlates to every subcategory. Why is that important?

Maybe you received an inquiry about how you and your organization have implemented its security controls. The inquiry is based on ISO or SP *800-53*, but wait a minute – you are using the CSF; how can those match up?

There is a matrix for each control and how that aligns with other frameworks. This is to assist in answering questions regarding the CSF as compared with other frameworks. It is also meant to assist you if you decide to adopt a different framework. The point is, if you start off with the CSF and decide to jump to another one, all is not lost. I am not, by any means, saying that you should start with the CSF and then naturally jump to a different framework. You can utilize the NIST CSF for all or a majority of the organization or partially implement the framework in the organization.

Business objectives do change, and with that, so do the cybersecurity controls that you implement. Let's take a look at the other frameworks referenced in the NIST CSF.

CIS

There have been several iterations of the CIS Controls. They were originally developed by the SANS Institute; however, they are now maintained by CIS. CIS has maintained that list for several years, changing the control families over time due to feedback from industry leaders. The list is constructed from the most to least important. In version 8, CIS developed **implementation groups (IGs)**, which define the controls to implement based on the resources an organization has.

CIS has also slimmed down the CIS Controls from 20 to 18. These categories comprise the following:

1. Inventory and Control of Enterprise Assets
2. Inventory and Control of Software Assets
3. Data Protection
4. Secure Configuration of Enterprise Assets and Software
5. Account Management
6. Access Control Management
7. Continuous Vulnerability Management

8. Audit Log Management

9. Email and Web Browser Protection

10. Malware Defenses

11. Data Recovery

12. Network Infrastructure Management

13. Network Monitoring and Defense

14. Security Awareness and Skill Training

15. Service Provider Management

16. Application Software Security

17. Incident Response Management

18. Penetration Testing

The framework has listed the controls from most to least important. This means that an organization should review its current processes for the discovery and documentation of IT resources within the environment. Quite honestly, if an organization performs a penetration test prior to the implementation of other controls, they are wasting time, money, and effort. A penetration test at the stage of getting your cybersecurity program going will provide you with information that you already know.

COBIT

COBIT 5 is based upon five different governance and management controls:

1. Meeting Stakeholder Needs

2. Covering the Enterprise End to End

3. Applying a Single, Integrated Framework

4. Enabling a Holistic Approach

5. Separating Governance from Management

COBIT is an enterprise governance and management framework used for IT. The framework takes you through how to implement the program and execute those plans. Then, you review the progress, evaluate your success criteria against the outcome, make a project plan for remediation, and start the process over again. This is an effective way to initiate a new project or for continuous improvement of IT.

ISO/IEC 27001

Created by ISO, ISO/IEC *27001* is an international standard used to baseline and secure IT assets and evaluate risk. The basis of the *27001* framework is to ensure that security controls are in place by adopting and applying the **confidentiality, integrity, and availability (CIA)** triad.

In addition to the CIA triad, it also specifies the use of an **information security management system (ISMS)**. The ISMS is used to capture security controls implemented within the environment. The CIA triad is defined by the following:

- **Confidentiality** – Restrict access to IT resources or information that is considered sensitive

- **Integrity** – Ensure that information has not been altered by anyone but the intended parties

- **Availability** – Information or IT resources are available as required by an organizational- or service-level agreement

Organizations and individuals can also get ISO *27001* certified. Organizations use the certification to prove to customers that they have a dedicated cybersecurity program in place. Individuals can also be certified, which will allow them to perform certification assessments for their company or other organizations.

NIST SP 800-53

One of the more widely used cybersecurity frameworks out there is NIST's SP *800-53*. The framework consists of 20 privacy and security control families with an estimated 1,000 separate controls. The US federal government is required by the **Federal Information Security Management Act (FISMA)** to implement the controls across all federal IT resources.

The control families are depicted in *Table 1.1*:

ID	Family	ID	Family
AC	Access Control	PE	Physical and Environmental Protection
AT	Awareness and Training	PL	Planning
AU	Audit and Accountability	PM	Program Management
CA	Assessment, Authorization, and Monitoring	PS	Personnel Control
CM	Configuration Management	PT	Personal Identifiable Information and Transparency
CP	Contingency Planning	RA	Risk Assessment
IA	Identification and Authentication	SA	System and Services Acquisition
IR	Incident Response	SC	System and Communications Protection
MA	Maintenance	SI	System and Information Integrity
MP	Media Protection	SR	Supply Chain Risk Management

Table 1.1 – NIST 800-53 control families

These are by no means an exhaustive list of cybersecurity frameworks, only the ones found in the *Informative References* section of the CSF. There are several frameworks that are just as important as the frameworks previously discussed. It is encouraged to review other frameworks and see if they align with your business needs and objectives.

NIST CSF success stories

Organizations have the freedom to use and implement the NIST CSF to best fit their needs. The beauty of the framework is in its flexibility in implementing the necessary cybersecurity controls. Plenty of organizations have achieved their goals of reducing overall cyber risk through its use, but do not take my word for it. The following is a set of success stories of other organizations that have implemented the CSF.

Lower Colorado River Authority

Serving the residents of Texas, the **Lower Colorado River Authority** (**LCRA**) has a tough job. LCRA ensures water coming from the river is safe to use for the millions of residents of that state. The river authority is considered a critical infrastructure and must ensure that its IT and **operational technology** (**OT**) are secured.

LCRA initially adopted NIST's SP *800-53* to implement cybersecurity controls. Due to its massive size, this caused serious problems with the framework rollout. LCRA required a framework that was agile and customizable due to its decentralization and the size of the organization. LCRA eventually abandoned SP *800-53* in favor of the CSF. This allowed them to apply a common framework across the entire organization. [*1*]

Biological Sciences Division – University of Chicago

Founded in 1890, the **University of Chicago** (**UoC**) has been serving its students for well over a century. The **Biological Sciences Division** (**BSD**) is one of the larger schools within UoC with 23 departments and 5,000 faculty and staff. The school requires multiple frameworks to be used to maintain compliance, including HIPAA and FedRAMP. Due to its decentralization, the school struggled to maintain a common security posture across all departments.

BSD gathered framework **subject-matter experts** (**SMEs**) to assist in the rollout of the framework. The organization developed a four-stage process that allowed them to achieve their goals in evaluating and reducing cyber risk effectively. Their four-stage approach involved the following:

1. Developing a current state profile
2. Performing a cybersecurity assessment
3. Creating a future state profile
4. Executing the roadmap

The team created a scoring system from 0-4 to establish a measurement of success between the two profiles. The BSD then went on to create training seminars for staff to better understand how to use the framework. [2]

Though these two success stories depict how they accomplished rolling out the NIST CSF across their organizations, how will you achieve the same goals? Where should you start, and how will you get there? The following chapters will answer those questions and much more.

Summary

In this chapter, we reviewed what a framework is and why it is important. Frameworks were developed to assist organizations in filling in the blanks of building a cybersecurity program. The NIST CSF is a framework that can be applied to your organization with little effort.

As cyber-attacks took hold during the early 2000s, we needed to rapidly increase our security posture. Cybersecurity frameworks were created to assist organizations in doing just that. Many may think that IT and cybersecurity are identical, but they are not. As we learned, cybersecurity has its own language and way of implementing solutions.

As we saw in the success stories, several organizations had come from other frameworks and began to use the CSF due to its flexibility in allowing for agility across multiple business functions.

In the next chapter, we will dive deeper into the CSF and review the framework core, tiers, and profiles. We will then look at how to evaluate and reduce risk. More to come!

References

1. *Cybersecurity Framework Success Story – Lower Colorado River Authority*:

   `https://www.nist.gov/system/files/documents/2021/10/26/LCRA%20`
   `CSF%20Success%20Story_Comments%20Incorporated%5B53%5D.pdf`

2. *Cybersecurity Framework Success Story – University of Chicago Biological Sciences Division*:

   `https://www.nist.gov/system/files/documents/2020/07/23/`
   `University%20of%20Chicago%20Success%20Story%20062920%20508.pdf`

2

NIST Cybersecurity Framework Fundamentals

In the previous chapter, we learned about what cybersecurity frameworks are and some of their differences. We know that cybersecurity frameworks help align us and our organizations to best practices. Frameworks provide a taxonomy and a common language for complex architecture and terminology.

We were briefly introduced to the NIST **Cybersecurity Framework** (**CSF**). The NIST CSF is a robust, agile framework that can be implemented in any organization. As we saw in the last chapter, several organizations have adopted other frameworks only to find out, months or years later, that the chosen framework does not meet their needs.

In this chapter, we will dive into the framework. We will look at the framework's Core, Tiers, and Profiles. We will discuss what each of these means so that you have a general understanding of the topics being discussed. In later chapters, we will go further into the Core and examine each of its six functions – govern, identify, protect, detect, respond, and recover.

This chapter will cover the following topics:

- The NIST framework
- Tiers
- Profiles

Let's dive in!

The NIST framework

This framework is made up of three separate modules – **Core**, **Tiers**, and **Profiles**. The Core is made up of six functions that are used to reduce cybersecurity risk in an organization:

- Govern
- Identify

- Protect

- Detect

- Respond

- Recover

Each control is numbered so that we easily know how the controls align together. As an example, an inventory of physical devices would be `ID.AM-01`, software inventory would be `ID.AM-02`, and so on:

Function.Category-subcategory

ID.AM-01

We will discuss the individual controls further in later chapters; for now, let's dive right into what each of the six functions means.

Govern

Govern is meant to establish governance throughout a cyber program. This is why the Govern function is at the center of all other functions. It is used to set a risk management strategy, policies, and standards, ensuring that these documents are well written and communicated. Govern is especially important when it comes to enterprise risk management.

This function also requires that you start discussing risk and risk management with everyone in your organization. Risk tolerance must start at the top with the executive leadership team and trickle down through middle management to your analysts. There should also be a feedback loop that allows risk mitigation efforts to ascend from the bottom up too. This is needed to better understand whether any risk tolerances that were established still work as intended.

Identify

The *Identify* function was created to help locate systems, software, and external services, such as **Software-as-a-Service (SaaS)**. This includes where your company is purchasing software and hardware and the use of third-party service(s). The identify function also exposes risk identification and management and helps create policies, standards, and procedures. These categories are used to assist in highlighting risks throughout the organization.

The first two control families of the *Critical Controls* provided by the Center for Internet Security also have visibility of hardware and software at the top of their list. An organization must have a grasp on inventorying all assets, both on-premises and in the cloud, to adequately protect them. Once they are identified, we can scan for vulnerabilities and apply security patches to keep IT resources secured.

An organization must document what is not in an environment for the following reasons:

- It helps identify rogue devices connected to a network

- It ensures ownership of a rogue device

- It reduces cyber risk in an environment

The Identity Function also requires a strategy for how you want to identify and record your SaaS applications for the same reasons.

Protect

As you might have guessed, the *Protect* function is all about safeguarding identities, data, baselining systems, maintenance, auditing, and logging. According to NIST, the protect function is also meant to limit or contain cybersecurity incidents.

In a 2023 study performed by BeyondTrust, the following are the top identity-based attacks that organizations face [1]:

- Phishing (62%)

- Inadequate management of privileges/privileged identities (37%)

- Third-party or supply chain attacks (37%)

- Insider attacks (22%)

- Man-in-the-middle attacks (18%)

It is no surprise that users and their digital identities are cybersecurity's weakest link. The protect function goes into detail about how to protect users by implementing a robust identity and access management system, along with security and awareness end-user training.

This function also ensures that data is secured. This is done using encryption, both in flight and at rest. At rest means the hard drives of laptops, desktops, servers, databases, and so on should be encrypted.

This can be easily accomplished by leveraging the built-in encryption tools used by each of the operating systems. Microsoft developed BitLocker, Apple has FileVault, and for Linux, there is **Linux Unified Key Setup (LUKS)** Each encryption scheme used by the operating system manufacturers has its advantages and disadvantages. Pay close attention to how you store the backup keys for each device that has been encrypted. Without storing the keys, you could lose all access to the information stored on the drive.

Detect

The *Detect* function is all about processes that you and your team develop to highlight threats, vulnerabilities, and viruses and monitor user behavior. This function is also about creating baselines of systems and the network to determine anomalies.

We start with anomalies and events. This is where baselines come in to discover unusual activity. To do this, monitoring needs to be in place. Typically, this is performed using the **Simple Network Monitoring Protocol** (**SNMP**). SNMP allows your team to poll usage statistics at a given interval (usually every minute), and those stats are stored in some type of flat file or database for historical review. Systems may also allow you to track malicious traffic and display it on a graph.

Another crucial step to take in monitoring is log aggregation. This involves a collection of logs from all systems in an environment, including firewalls, IT systems, network devices, and databases. This will allow you to monitor systems and services to detect malicious activity throughout the environment.

Lastly, we need to document detection processes and establish roles and responsibilities. This is a necessary step to determine who is responsible for detecting and remediating an incident if one occurs.

Respond

How do we respond to an incident? Who is responsible for what? How are events communicated? This will require the creation of an incident response and communication plan. Not all incidents need to be communicated; however, you will need a plan in place for who to speak with and when.

Analysis of an incident is also part of the *Respond* function. This requires knowing the types of threats that are out there, especially those that are executed in the wild. There are plenty of threat intelligence lists to choose from. Some you must pay for, and some are generally free to consume. The **Cybersecurity and Infrastructure Security Agency** (**CISA**) produces a list of known exploits that are actively used in the wild, called the **Known Exploited Vulnerabilities** (**KEV**). This is a free service that sends out email notifications and produces lists of known exploits on its website.

Documentation is key to the success of this function. You will not only need to document policies and standards for how to respond to an incident; you will also need to document everything during the event. This involves recording the response to the incident so that you can respond faster to it the next time, which is performed through an after-action review.

Recover

There are only two categories in the *Recover* function – *Incident Recover Plan Execution* and *Incident Recovery Communication*. While the respond function also contains a communication category, this control deals with communication with external stakeholders.

When an incident occurs, you must follow the steps laid out in the response plan. If you or your team did not follow the steps, why? Was the plan not well formed for the incident? Were there steps missing? This all gets discussed during the after-action review to make improvements to the plan itself.

An after-action review or a lessons-learned activity is used as part of your continuous improvement process. After an incident has occurred, the team is pulled together to hold one of these sessions. This is the last step in your incident response. An after-action review allows the **Security Incident Response Team** (**SIRT**) to praise one another on a job well done. However, it is also a time to vent frustrations as to what went wrong during the incident.

An after-action review is a "*what happens in Vegas stays in Vegas!*" scenario (this famous slogan is used in many Las Vegas commercials) It is just as essential to vent frustrations, as it is the only way the team will learn from their mistakes.

There will be more discussion of functions and their control families in later chapters. It is important to understand how functions, categories, and subcategories are grouped into control families. Some duplications of controls do occur in the framework – for instance, *communication* is referenced twice in the functions. There is a distinction between the two functions of each control that must be understood.

The next section will cover how to apply tiers to each of these controls so that you have a way to gauge your cybersecurity program.

Tiers

When rolling out a new program, we must first understand where they are at (the current state) and where they intend to go (the future state). While framework profiles are used to determine current and future states, we need to first assess the current state. We will focus more on performing these types of assessments later in this chapter. We must first understand how to rank our program against the framework.

Auditing firms tend to rank the NIST CSF on a maturity ranking by leveraging the **Capability Maturity Model Integration** (**CMMI**). This changes the framework's original intention in evaluating and reducing risks. There are some similarities between the framework tiers and CMMI. Most of the similarities come in the form of documentation and official organizational policies. However, this was not the intent of the framework.

In fact, the framework specifically states that it is not intended to be evaluated as a maturity model. This is not to say that maturity should not be part of the evaluation; it should. In fact, you will see similarities between the framework tiers and the CMMI. However, we will be staying as true to the intent of the framework as possible, as its intent is to reduce overall cyber risk.

There are plenty of criteria that go into evaluating your current environment and how it aligns with the framework tiers. The framework score values are between tier 1 (partial) and tier 4 (adaptive). This will help visualize what controls are missing and highlight where improvements are needed.

There are requirements that must be met to evaluate your program for the next tier. The criteria are mentioned in the following sub-categories.

The application of tiers

Let's take a look at the four different tiers and how they reduce risk:

- **Tier 1 - partial**:

  - **Cybersecurity risk governance**: Risk strategy and prioritization of objectives and threats are ad hoc at best.

  - **Cybersecurity risk management**: An organization does not have the necessary processes in place and handles risk on a case-by-case basis. The organization also has a lack of understanding of its role in the supply chain and how third parties can affect it. The organization also does not have a standardized method for sharing cyber risk-related information.

- **Tier 2 – risk-informed**:

  - **Cybersecurity risk governance**: The management of risk is approved by management; however, it may not be organizational-wide. The prioritization of cyber projects is directly related to the organization, policies, standards, or business requirements.

  - **Cybersecurity risk management**: There is a departmental view of cyber risks, however, it is localized and not throughout the organization. Threat information is shared internally but not consistently. The organization is also aware of the cybersecurity risks associated with third parties but has an inconsistent workflow.

- **Tier 3 – repeatable**:

  - **Cybersecurity risk governance**: Risk management is approved by management but not necessarily for an entire organization. Prioritization of cyber needs is directly informed by external risk intel and business requirements.

  - **Cybersecurity risk management**: There is an organizational understanding of cyber risks; however, there is no organizational-wide policy for how to deal with it. Cyber risk information is shared on an irregular basis, and an organization is aware of the third parties it does business with; however, there is not a consistent method for interaction.

- **Tier 4 – adaptive**:

  - **Cybersecurity risk governance**: There is an organizational-wide method to manage cyber risks. The relationships between policies and procedures that address cyber risk are implemented consistently. Cyber risk management is ingrained in the organizational culture.

  - **Cybersecurity risk management**: An organization implements its cyber risk program in the current threat landscape. This allows an adaptive approach to managing cyber risk. Lessons-learned activities are performed consistently to ensure that the program is up to date and a team is adaptive to new threats.

As we can see, there are similarities between the framework tiers and the CMMI model. However, while there are similarities, there are also plenty of differences – take, for instance, the cybersecurity risk management scenarios. These relate to how an organization handles business with its upstream and downstream providers. It is just as critical to know and understand how the organization plays a bigger role in a sector's ecosystem. This helps build resiliency in how the business operates.

The tiers will play a significant role in how you grade yourself when performing an assessment. This assessment is used to understand your current security posture and develop a future state or strategic roadmap. This roadmap is used to plan for future projects that will reduce cyber risk for an organization. Profiles are a way to understand the current state of risk and how you want to reduce it.

Next, we look at how to build profiles and learn how they reduce risk.

Continuous improvement

Continuous improvement is necessary for any cybersecurity program. As you can see from the tiers overview, to improve or advance in a tiering structure, you must also improve your organizational processes. To do this, we will review the **Deming cycle**.

In the 1950s, a quality control engineer by the name of William Deming created the concept of **Plan, Do, Check, and Act** (**PDCA**). Although PDCA was originally used to improve business processes, we can also use this philosophy to improve our cybersecurity program. In *Figure 2.1*, you can see the Deming cycle in a continuous loop. This cycle allows you to plan for upcoming projects, go through the implementation phase, and then gather information about what did and did not work. Once that information has been collected, we go through the planning phase again:

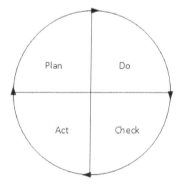

Figure 2.1 – The Deming cycle

This is what the stages in the Deming cycle consist of:

1. **Plan**: This is the planning phase of a new project. We gather the correct stakeholders together to design a solution intended to reduce cyber risk. We evaluate and discover discrepancies between the current and future states (more to come) and plan how we want to reduce cyber

risk. During this phase, you may also want to begin the purchase of software and hardware or schedule the assistance of a trusted third party to assist in their implementation.

You should also document your test plans so that you and your team know what is in and out of scope for a project. This could also be used as a project charter to implement or modify a system resource.

2. **Do**: In this phase, you do the work. This is where you begin the implementation of new systems and processes or modify existing ones. We review the test plan to ensure that the controls that were laid out are installed and configured accordingly.

3. **Check**: We now must check whether the improvements or mitigations that were put in place work as intended. The team begins testing the new controls to ensure that the desired state is what was intended. We test **Key Performance Indicators** (**KPIs**) to ensure that the metrics produced are well within the operational and service level agreements.

    While the check phase is performed during a given cycle, there should be ongoing checks of security controls to ensure that they meet specific metrics. You should continuously check the controls to ensure that they work properly and that they finish well within expected completion times.

4. **Act**: During the act phase, you collect all of the metrics and determine the next step. If the mitigations that were put in place work as intended, great! Move on to the next issue and run through the cycle again. If not, then we need to understand what was implemented, how it was implemented, and reevaluate our cyber risk posture.

    This could mean that mitigation reduced the risk by, say, 75%, but you were aiming to reduce it by 85%, giving you a delta of 10%. You now review what was implemented and what didn't work as intended, you devise a new mitigation plan, and the cycle starts all over again.

PDCA is used to improve many aspects of your program – from evaluating new IT systems and cybersecurity controls to developing policies, standards, and procedures. This method can be used anywhere within your program.

Profiles

We need a way to evaluate the overall risk posture of an organization. To do this successfully, we must understand the current state of the cybersecurity program and determine where we intend the program to go. This can sometimes be simple, especially when you currently work for the organization. However, if you are a newly hired employee, you will need to perform an assessment or have one performed for you first.

The risk assessment provides several benefits. First, it helps you build relationships with your new coworkers. Building relationships should be the first objective when entering a new organization. This allows you to get acquainted with the executive leadership team, the IT team, and the incident response team. This is also the time when you have conversations to better understand the IT and security history of the company.

Second, performing the assessment will give you a background of the currently implemented controls. These conversations will provide insight into the technology stack, how it was implemented, and the mitigating controls that were placed on the IT resource. Assessments can also answer questions about how risk is calculated and what the overall risk appetite is.

Performing an assessment

There are several ways to perform an assessment. We can do it ourselves, which is called a first-party assessment, or have one performed for us, called a third-party assessment. Both have their advantages and disadvantages.

Third-party assessments

Let's start with third-party assessments. A third-party assessor is a company that was hired to perform a risk assessment on your behalf. These can sometimes be the easiest to do; however, it is the most expensive option. Impact assessments against the CSF can sometimes cost tens if not hundreds of thousands of dollars. This all depends on the scope and size of an organization.

This might be the best option if you have never performed an assessment before. In performing a third-party assessment, you will work with a team of **governance, risk, and compliance** (**GRC**) analysts. These analysts will review all your documentation, such as policies, standards, procedures, and network and application flow diagrams, and gather evidence to back up your processes.

In addition to collecting evidence, you, your team, and executive leadership will be asked a series of questions about your people, processes, and technology. These questions are used in conjunction with the provided evidence to better understand the maturity of your security program. These questions will be centered around the implemented controls and how they align both with business requirements and the framework itself.

Third-party assessors will provide a report at the end of the assessment. This report will provide a score based on your current posture. In many instances, the assessment firm will also provide a redacted report that can be sent to your third parties, allowing them to better understand the organizational security posture too.

Third parties also provide a non-biased assessment. When performing first-party assessments, there is a tendency to score yourself better on an implemented control than you should have. We are all guilty of it. However, if you assess your organization, remember to remove these biases from your scores.

If you are feeling up for learning new skills, or have performed assessments in the past, you may want to perform the assessment yourself. This is called a first-party assessment.

First-party assessments

First-party assessments are the least expensive and can be fun, exciting, and, if you have never performed one before, maybe a little intimidating. There are a lot of benefits to performing a first-party assessment. For instance, you get to control the time, the questions, or anything else about the assessment process.

However, there are key success criteria that you should be aware of. For instance, one key aspect is listening. When you are in the seat asking assessment questions, be cognizant of the environment and the people around you. Pay special attention to side conversations and body language. This can sometimes lead to additional information that can assist in your evaluation.

The process can differ, depending on whether you are a new hire or have been with a company for some time. For instance, if are a long-term employee, then you may be able to score yourself without performing an assessment first. If you are new to the organization, I would perform an assessment first before scoring yourself and creating a current state profile.

To perform the assessment, I suggest following these steps.

The engagement letter

First, you need a letter of engagement. This gives you permission to perform an assessment. The letter should state the intent of the engagement and any scans that may be required to gather information, and it should request permission to perform the duties of the assessment.

There may be times when a scan does not perform the way that you intended it to. This could impact system performance or render a system inoperable. The engagement letter is also your *get out of jail free card*, meaning that an executive member permitted you to perform the scans and assessment.

Project initiation

Once you have an engagement letter signed by a member of the executive team, it is time to begin the assessment and start collecting evidence. This includes policies, standards, procedures, network diagrams, and other internal documents to review. Gathering this information will help you understand the business, and it will also provide insight into the technology being used so that you can direct the conversation toward specific security and IT-related systems.

This is also the time to start your scans. There are plenty of paid-for and open source tools that can be used for scanning. The **Center for Internet Security** (**CIS**) has several benchmarks that can be used to harden systems. Running a CIS scan is helpful in determining the configuration settings of an IT resource. Once scanned, the tool will generate a pass/fail report that you can use to determine the correct settings for your environment.

If you are technically inclined, several open source tools can be used. For instance, you can gain a lot of information from the **Domain Name System** (**DNS**). With DNS, you can discover who their email provider is, where their DNS records are located, and the geographic locations of IT resources based on an IP address. Many SaaS providers require a customer to place a TXT record in their DNS. This can also provide insight into other services that an organization may be using.

DNSEnum, another open source tool, can be used to discover DNS entries for a particular domain. You can then determine various IT resources that are being used by a company. As an example, you could determine the type of firewall the company has by picking up clues such as `vpn.example.com`.

Network Mapper (NMAP) is a tool that can be used to discover an IT resource on a network. NMAP will allow you to perform ICMP or PING scans across a network to discover live hosts. You can also use it to discover open ports and services running on a server.

NMAP will also try to detect the type of device and operating system on an IT resource. For instance, when scanning a Microsoft Windows 2019 server, you would receive the following message:

```
Service Info: OS: Windows; CPE: cpe:/o:microsoft:windows
```

Conversely, if you were to scan a Linux system, you would see this:

```
OS CPE: cpe:/o:linux:linux_kernel:2.6.32
```

However, you may also run into this message:

```
Too many fingerprints match this host to give specific OS details
```

This message occurs when it cannot determine an operating system or its version.

These scans do not always get the correct version of the operating system. For example, the Linux system scan thought the system had a 2.6.32 kernel, whereas the system was running 6.1.0. While not necessarily accurate, it does determine the overall operating system type.

I understand that these techniques can be used for good and bad intentions. However, I believe that when they are used for good, these tools provide valuable insight into the environment that you are assessing.

Now that we have reviewed the policy documents, studied the network diagrams, and run our scans, it is time to do the questionnaire.

Performing the assessment

Now, it is time to perform the questionnaire portion of the assessment. Many first and third-party questionnaires are performed, either in person or through virtual meetings. However, you can also send out the questionnaire and have the other party fill it out. This is less involved and may not receive the results that you are looking for.

When conducting an assessment in person, offer the personal touch when asking how an organization is meeting the control objective. I typically write out the question and ask it in such a way that it makes sense to the receiving party. As an example, `PR.DS-01` states, "*The confidentiality, integrity, and availability of data-at-rest are protected.*" What does that mean? Protected from what?

That is a very open-ended question! Rephrase it to make sense, such as, *"How are you protecting the data? Is the data encrypted? Are you mapping your data flows and know where sensitive data resides?"* These are just a few of the questions that pertain to this control. You are probably asking yourself, *"How would I know that the control pertains to all of these questions?"* If you ever need clarification, the best place to check is in the information references for the control.

PR.DS-01 is referenced to CIS controls 13 and 14. Control 13 pertains to data protection, while 14 is how you control access to data. Each control family in CIS also has sub-controls. However, if you ever have a question about a control from the CSF, look at the referenced documents for more clarity.

Wrap up the assessment

Once the questionnaire portion of the assessment is wrapped up and you have collected all the evidence, it is time to score it. When tallying up the scores, remember to align the answers and the evidence to the tiers that we previously discussed. While evaluating the answers, consider the risk profile, how an organization plans to reduce cyber risk, and how the business interacts with its upstream and downstream providers for that control.

These scores help in understanding what your overall cyber risk is and where to focus your energy. For example, review *Table 2.1*:

Function	Category	Subcategory	Score
Respond	RS.AN	RS.AN-03	25
		RS.AN-06	50
		RS.AN-07	25
		RS.AN-08	75
Average subcategory score			43.75

Table 2.1 – An NIST CSF analysis category

The average score for the RS.AN category is 43.75. This places your overall tier level at 2. What score should you be aiming for? Well, that depends on your organization and the level of risk you are willing to accept. The sweet spot in all of this, in my opinion, is tier 3. This means that an organization has policies, standards, and procedures that are approved either by management or are organizational-wide, the business understands its role in the larger ecosystem, and resiliency is in place.

The exit interview

The exit interview is the last step in the assessment process, as it is used to report on findings. Findings are missing or inadequate controls found in IT resources, policy documents, or diagrams. As the lead assessor, it is your responsibility to create a report and present it to key stakeholders within an organization.

The report should detail the findings, evidence collected, and how employees responded to the questions. Findings can be missing controls or controls that do not meet expectations or standards. For example, during the assessment, you may have determined that four out of the six IT resources had antivirus software installed, while another resource had it installed but was not receiving updates. These findings are then put into a **Plan of Action and Milestones** (or a project plan) for remediation.

Findings are not just for configuration items set on IT resources; they can also come in written documents. Policy documents are hard to write, and writing good policies is even harder. Policy documents should be written so that a new analyst or engineer can read the document and know exactly what to do and how to do it. You also need to have an IT policy document life cycle in place to review and approve IT policy documents.

Findings in policy documents are not as easy as, say, finding an issue with an IT resource. It does take skill to read and understand a document's intentions and poke holes in it. Maybe you missed a crucial step in a procedure or there's an encryption standard that states to use legacy protocols. These should be considered reportable findings and highlighted during the exit interview process.

As we finalize the exit interview process, we can now create the current state and future state profiles. The current state is where you are currently in your cybersecurity program, and the future state is where you see an organization going in the not-so-distant future.

The current state

A current state profile is based on an organization's alignment with the CSF at a particular moment. This alignment considers the configurations of IT resources, policy documents, and practices. This is a current snapshot of your overall program. The current state also depicts the overall cyber risk posture of the organization. The work has already been completed through your presentation during the exit interview process. Now, it is time to develop your strategic roadmap.

The future state

We have put in all the hard work in the assessment phase, and we reported our findings to the executive leadership team; now, it is time to develop our future state. The future state profile depicts where you plan to take your cybersecurity program over the next two to five years. This is your strategy to reduce organizational cyber risk to acceptable levels.

Now is the time when you put together a project plan, or **Plan of Action and Milestones (POA&M)**. This is the plan you intend to develop to remediate the findings from the report. You will need to sit down with the leadership team to better understand their objectives and what they consider risky. This is your time to evaluate an environment and decide what is low-hanging fruit, eliminating it quickly while you put together larger POA&Ms for major projects.

Summary

The NIST CSF is packed with great information to set up your cybersecurity and risk management programs. The core of the framework, made up of six functions, its categories, and subcategory controls, is used to reduce cyber risk in your organization. The framework will assist you and your team in elevating your posture and maturing a program.

While many score the NIST CSF against a maturity model, it should be evaluated against risk. This is the true intent of the CSF and is true for other frameworks as well. Risk is further evaluated in three separate categories – risk management processes, integrated risk management, and external participation. When evaluating an organization against the framework tiers, remember that we are evaluating against risk and its place in a greater ecosystem.

Is resiliency built into a design? Are the policy documents aligned with business objectives? Does documentation come from an organization, or is it localized within a department? These are all questions that should be asked during the evaluation.

As you evaluate those questions, ensure that they meet the requirements from the framework tiers – from tier 1, where barely anything exists, to tier 4, where everything is adaptable and optimized for efficiency. Remember that tier 3 is really the sweet spot for your program. While tier 4 may be the pinnacle of efficiency, sometimes this cannot be achieved due to its expense. Expense may not be defined by monetary value either; it can also involve personnel resources.

Profiles are used to understand where you are currently in your program and where you strive to be in the next three to five years. A current state profile depicts the state of a cybersecurity program at a given time. The future state profile is your strategy for where you plan to take the program. As you continue to work through your strategy, remember to develop a POA&M to plan your projects.

In the following chapters, we will review the six functions and how you can use them to align your cybersecurity program.

References

1. https://www.beyondtrust.com/blog/entry/the-state-of-identity-security-identity-based-threats-breaches-security-best-practices

Part 2: NIST Cybersecurity Framework Functions

The framework consists of six different functions, all of which are designed to reduce cyber risk within an organization. At the center of it all is *Govern*, which directs all the other functions within the framework. This part walks you through identifying assets, detecting threats, and recovering from an event.

This part has the following chapters:

- *Chapter 3, Govern*
- *Chapter 4, Identify*
- *Chapter 5, Protect*
- *Chapter 6, Detect*
- *Chapter 7, Respond*
- *Chapter 8, Recover*

3
Govern

In the previous chapter, we took a look at the NIST **Cybersecurity Framework (CSF)** [*1*] and its three components: **Core**, **Tiers**, and **Profiles**. We learned that the Core is made up of six different functions: **Govern**, **Identify**, **Protect**, **Detect**, **Respond**, and **Recover**. Each of these functions pertains to different control objectives that are used to reduce cyber risk.

We apply tiers, or a score, to each of the sub-categories to better understand our risk posture. Ranging from 1 to 4, each tier increases from little evaluation of risk to continuous evaluation and improvement. We also learned how to apply the **Deming cycle** to our processes so that they can advance from a lower tier to a higher tier.

Lastly, we created profiles to understand where the security program is currently, and where we plan to take it in the next 3 to 5 years. Remember, we shouldn't take a *cheeky box* approach to cybersecurity. It's a program, one that shouldn't just fill a box and move on. It needs dedicated people, processes, and technology to ensure the program protects the organization while reducing cyber risk.

This chapter will cover the **Govern function**. Govern, which is a new function category for CSF 2.0, is at the heart of pretty much all of the other functions in the framework. At its core, Govern is meant to align the cyber program with business objectives. This includes understanding and promoting the business's mission statement, how to determine risk and establish a risk management threshold, and a considerable amount of documentation around roles and responsibilities.

In this chapter, we will cover the following topics:

- Organizational context
- Risk management strategy
- Roles, responsibilities, and authorities
- Policy
- Oversight
- **Cybersecurity supply chain risk management (C-SCRM)**

So, let's take a closer look at the newest function: Govern!

Technical requirements

As we progress through the six functions in this book, each chapter will be structured around the controls and sub-controls in the framework. The sub-controls will include both the sub-control's identifier and its objective. Each objective is referenced from the framework directly to not draw confusion between the book and the framework. For additional information on the framework, please look at the *References* section at the end of this chapter.

Organizational context (GV.OC)

Organizational context is meant to align yourself and your cyber program with business objectives. Does the program fall in or out of the core business objectives? How are risks identified and communicated to key stakeholders? Maybe your business also requires that you follow other frameworks or regulatory requirements. How will that affect your program?

GC.OC-01

> *The organizational mission is understood and informs cybersecurity risk management.*

Chances are your organization has a mission and vision statement, but do you know what they are? Mission and vision statements are meant to help drive the purpose of the company. They are also meant to be public-facing so that their customers, even shareholders, can understand and know what the company strives for.

A mission statement is a short statement that mentions why the company is in business and how it defines its goals and values. These statements do not have to be very long; in fact, some of the largest organizations in the world have mission statements that are one to two sentences in length. Let's take a look at a few:

- *"To empower every person and organization on the planet to achieve more."* – Microsoft.
- *"To bring the best user experience to customers through innovative hardware, software, and services."* – Apple.
- *"To be the Earth's most customer-centric company."* – Amazon.

As you can see, each of these statements is just a single sentence long, concise, and to the point. Vision statements are no different. Let's take a look at the vision statements for the same three companies.

- *"To help people and businesses throughout the world realize their full potential."* – Microsoft.
- *"To make the best products on Earth and to leave the world better than we found it."* – Apple.
- *"To become Earth's best employer and Earth's safest place to work."* – Amazon.

Vision statements are meant to strive or achieve a goal. This goal can either be in a short or long-term period or just over the lifetime of the company. Regardless, it is meant to state what the company intends to achieve in the future.

Does your cyber program align with any of these statements? Could you align your program with the statements mentioned previously? It is also not uncommon for cyber programs to also have a mission and vision statement – many do. The key here is to understand the overall business objectives and align your program so that you don't hinder it from obtaining those objectives.

GV.OC-02

Internal and external stakeholders are understood, and their needs and expectations regarding cybersecurity risk management are understood and considered.

Many organizations and security departments like to hold the "No!" sign. This means that whatever you do as an organization, you are bound to hear no from the security department. "We have to protect the kids from running with scissors!" This hinders the business from doing its job fulfilling customer or other stakeholder needs.

Any program, whether it is cyber-related or not, must have buy-in from the top; otherwise, the program will go nowhere. It is time to understand who your stakeholders are and understand them, not only professionally but also personally. This is a time when you need to build relationships with all stakeholders.

Ask questions during stakeholder meetings so that you can understand who they are and what makes them tick. Do they understand cyber-related concepts and know what their risk tolerance is? If not, have these conversations so that you know where they stand on issues related to the cloud, artificial intelligence, multi-factor authentication, and policies and standards.

As you have these conversations, get to know them on a personal level too. This will help comfort both you and the others in the group so that they feel at ease when bringing an issue to you. You should also hold one-on-one conversations with your employees; these are not just meant for executives. This is all meant to drive conversations around risk and risk appetite.

You will also need to build relationships with external stakeholders. These include law enforcement, vendors, or even peers within the cyber community. These relationships are meant to assist you in a time of crisis. There are plenty of **Information Sharing and Analysis Centers (ISACs)** that you may be able to be part of. Non-profits along with state and local governments can be a part of the Multi-State ISAC. Automotive manufacturers have the Auto ISAC and there is even a financial services ISAC that financial organizations can be a part of.

ISACs are a great resource in that they share much-needed threat intelligence with their members. This threat intelligence can be useful, especially with sector-specific organizations, to help promote cybersecurity best practices when dealing with threats and vulnerabilities that affect those organizations.

GV.OC-03

Legal, regulatory, and contractual requirements regarding cybersecurity – including privacy and civil liberties obligations – are understood and managed.

So, you have settled on leveraging the NIST CSF as your baseline framework. Your organization may also have other legal and regulatory compliance requirements on top of the CSF. For example, **human resources (HR)** may have to abide by the **Health Insurance Portability and Accountability Act (HIPAA)**, finance may have to abide by the **Payment Card Industry Data Security Standard (PCI DSS)**, or the organizational overall might even have to abide by international regulatory requirements such as the **General Data Protection Regulation (GDPR)**.

In *GV.OC-02*, we talked about building relationships with key stakeholders – this is why. The key stakeholders or the **executive leadership team (ELT)** should know about these types of compliance requirements and where the organization conducts business. If someone on the ELT mentions that a department takes credit cards for business transactions, then you should automatically think about PCI. If health records are in your environment, then you must follow the privacy and data security protections in HIPAA. But how do you know where to apply the controls?

For example, PCI DSS 4.0 states that you must have a minimum of 12 characters for passwords, but your company standard is 10; which do you choose? For these scenarios, you must choose the most stringent of the control. In this instance, you would have to apply the 12-character password to all systems that process, store, or transmit credit card information. You may also have requirements for multi-factor authentication for remote administration of systems or IT resources. This too will affect how you authenticate to these systems.

In many instances, if you do not abide by these requirements, then you'll face penalties and fines. In several instances, the ability to perform such an action could be taken away for negligence. Try to explain to your ELT why you can no longer take credit card transactions because you failed your last PCI assessment.

You should understand what types of regulatory requirements you may have for your organization and how they apply to cyber and IT overall. This will not only make you better at what you do, but it will enable the organization to continue to conduct business with its customers.

GV.OC-04

Critical objectives, capabilities, and services that external stakeholders depend on or expect from the organization are understood and communicated.

As we will see in the **Identify** function, inventorying IT resources is a critical part of cybersecurity. First, we must identify what we have in the environment and then apply criticality labels to those assets. Those Identify function controls will have a direct impact on how you accomplish this goal.

We need to identify our assets, apply criticality labels, and ensure that we are also calculating the risk of losing that asset. For example, let's say you have a web server that is selling products and services to your customers. If that system were to go down for some reason, how would that impact your company and your external customers?

Amazon, one of the world's largest retailers, experienced an outage in 2013 that cost the company an estimated $66,240 per minute or nearly $2 million for its duration [2]. Could your company experience an outage like that? Most of us would say no as it would immediately put us out of business.

This control is meant to highlight the criticality of the systems and services you provide. Hospitals are the same, where a ransomware attack can bring down emergency and operating rooms, denying customers critical care. How will an outage affect you and your customers?

You can qualitatively calculate the criticality of an IT resource by understanding the **confidentiality, integrity, and availability (CIA)** of the resource. By applying a watermark of low, moderate, or high to the CIA triad, it can help you understand how critical the system is.

For example, if you decide to apply a high watermark for availability, you will want to look at **high availability (HA)** to build redundancy for the resource. If confidentiality and integrity of the data are moderate because you are dealing with health records, then more controls will be placed on ensuring the information stays within the confines of the corporate network and employees.

NIST has another class of documentation called the **Federal Information Processing Standards (FIPS)**. In this documentation, you will find a document called **FIPS 199**, which goes into great detail about how the CIA can be calculated, as well as the definitions of each watermark that can be applied to the CIA triad [3].

GV.OC-05

Outcomes, capabilities, and services that the organization depends on are understood and communicated.

Inventorying internal resources is just a part of your overall need for identifying the resources you have. It is also critical to inventory your external resources. This includes inventorying the software and hardware that's used. Categorize these assets in a tiering structure so that you know their importance to your organization.

Also, consider the **cloud service providers (CSPs)** the external third party is using. Many providers have their accreditations on their websites, promoting the security controls that were implemented on the assets. Be sure to review these documents yearly to ensure that the provider is maintaining a level of security that is within the organization's risk levels.

From mission and vision statements to learning the various types of compliance requirements needed to successfully run your program, they all have their nuances for what is needed when evaluating cyber risk. The next control family we'll consider discusses how a risk management strategy can be implemented in your organization.

Risk management strategy (GV.RM)

While risk identification may not start at the top of the organization, the discussion around it should. The ELT must have these discussions regarding how the organization wants to manage and eliminate the risks associated with doing business. This includes managing assets both internal and external to the organization. This also draws attention to the need for enterprise risk management, which will be discussed later in this section.

GV.RM-01

Risk management objectives are established and agreed to by organizational stakeholders.

In *Chapter 2*, we discussed building profiles for current and future state objectives. These plans should be updated at least annually to project the overall strategy being used to minimize cyber risk. Evaluating the current and future states can better prepare you for updating your overall cyber strategy and keep you on track for what you intend to accomplish.

This does not mean that risk should be taken out of this objective. Have discussions with senior leaders or the ELT to ensure that the cyber initiatives you intend to work on over the next 6 to 12 months align with the overall business goals and objectives that need to be met.

You also need to make these measurable, meaning that you must have good metrics to back up what you are performing. Can you measure the amount of vulnerabilities being remediated? How does your cybersecurity awareness and training measure up to industry standards? Without measurable goals and objectives, how will you be able to measure the successes that you accomplished by implementing these programs?

GV.RM-02

Risk appetite and risk tolerance statements are established, communicated, and maintained.

We will discuss how to develop a policy management program later in this book; however, it is important to note that risk tolerance must be written and communicated with stakeholders. Much like the tiers and how we will evaluate our risk against those tiers, risk tolerance should be evaluated much the same way.

Without having these discussions around risk tolerance and getting assumptions or knowns down on paper, your staff may not know how to handle risk. Assumptions for how the ELT wants to handle risk should then immediately flow downward throughout the organization so that they too know how to handle risk when it comes up.

Also, build metrics for how risk was identified and resolved. Was the risk fully remediated or was there residual risk left over? How do you handle the residual risk and how are you recording it for future evaluations? Each asset or IT resource should have a risk register that accompanies it. This risk register is used to record the identified risks in the environment and build a project plan for how you intend to remediate those risks.

Lastly, while you write down the identified risks and how you intend to remediate them, build metrics around this. This will help you build the story of how you are tackling organizational risk throughout the organization. You can also get into detail about what was and wasn't working when you were trying to eliminate or reduce that risk. Not all risks can be eliminated, and it is impossible to fully reduce all risks to zero. However, the plans for reducing this risk are important and the story you tell others will make or break your program.

GV.RM-03

Cyber risk management activities and outcomes are included in enterprise risk management processes.

If your organization does not already have a way of reducing risk, you will need to build one. When evaluating risk on an IT resource, you could have a risk register per resource, scoped environment, or the entire IT infrastructure. The point here is, how are you identifying and promoting that identification of risk to the rest of the organization?

At a minimum, a risk register should do the following:

- Describe the asset
- Identify the risk
- Specify the likelihood of the risk being exploited
- Specify who is responsible for remediating the risk
- Specify how much it will cost – **CapEx/OpEx**
- Specify planned remediation timelines
- Specify the ownership of the remediation

I highly suggest keeping a risk register for each scoped environment. This way, it minimizes the number of risks that you must search through when looking at the resource. I also highly recommend building an enterprise risk register that not only encompasses the risks identified for the scoped area but also showcases all the risks identified in the organization.

Creating an enterprise risk register will bring in all of the identified risks for each scoped environment. The highest-ranked risks should be at the top of the enterprise risk register for all IT resources in the environment. This will help you identify the risks associated with everything, not just a couple of assets that you focused on.

Include risks from other departments as well. Regulatory and reputational risks are often overlooked when developing a risk register. As we will see in later chapters, reputational risk is often hard to remediate as you are trying to promote yourself as a secure organization after a breach or other mishap.

GV.RM-04

A strategic direction that describes appropriate risk response options is established and communicated.

Once a risk has been identified, you must do something about it. We previously discussed the need to implement policies and standards for how to handle risk. However, how do we accept or even transfer the risk if we don't intend to perform any further mitigations to eliminate the risk?

Organizations should have a way of accepting the risk posed to the organization. There should be an approval process that allows those in the ELT to review and either accept, mitigate, transfer, or avoid the risk altogether. If risks are mitigated, great – the job is almost complete. If there are residual risks, or risks that the ELT will just accept, there must be an approval process.

This can be accomplished by either gathering signatures or using some type of stamp of approval from an ELT member stating that the risk poses little to no threat to the organization. What if a risk is unavoidable? Many organizations will also purchase cyber insurance to transfer that risk to a third party. You should have these discussions with the insurance provider – often, their risk tolerance levels are lower than your organization. Remember, the insurance company is also on the hook if/ when something happens to your organization. They, like your organization, are in the business of making money, not losing it.

GV.RM-05

Lines of communication across the organization are established for cybersecurity risks, including risks from suppliers and other third parties.

Lines of communication should be open when discussing cyber risk in the organization. While identifying cyber risk and how we communicate that risk starts at the top, it must flow downward throughout the organization. Your enterprise architecture team, engineers, and analysts are the ones who are implementing the controls and ensuring that the risk is removed from the environment.

There must be a feedback loop from the engineers and analysts that flows back up to the top so that the ELT can understand any shortcomings. Maybe a particular remediation cannot be accomplished because you lack a certain control, or the control that you do have can't resolve it due to a lacking feature. This must be communicated and discussed to ensure that all parties involved are working toward a common goal.

Does your plan also include how to communicate and respond to an incident that may have occurred in a different area or department in the organization? For example, you tell employees not to tailgate each other when coming into the building. However, this would require that you have an open communication policy if someone identifies that this has occurred. In that plan, you should have who to contact and when so that the employees know what to do. Maybe you have the employee contact their immediate supervisor or manager when an isolated incident occurs, and it is escalated to your CISO if this happens multiple times.

This also requires that your third-party vendors and suppliers do the same thing. Ensure that you have contact information regarding how to respond if/when that vendor has an issue. Often, when partnering with another provider, they will require that you have their contact information in your incident response call tree so that you know who to contact when something does come up.

GV.RM-06

A standardized method for calculating, documenting, categorizing, and prioritizing cybersecurity risks is established and communicated.

Risk is often calculated using the following formula:

Risk = Likelihood * Impact

These risk scores should also be included in the risk register discussed previously. This risk calculation will help identify the most important risks and prioritize them for remediation efforts.

How do you prioritize the use of these numbers and their overall risk to the organization? This is often less understood than just using the calculations alone. However, you should not only prioritize based upon the calculated risk number in addition to who may have access to the resource. For example, let's say that you have several high-ranking risks on an internal asset that's behind two different firewalls and only 10 people can access it. You also have a high-ranking risk and several moderate risks on an asset that's public-facing. Which one should you remediate first?

This question is posed all the time and many people miss its significance. I once had a manager explain this to a group of junior analysts. Years ago, back before the internet, people had to drive to a bank and either go inside or use the drive-through for their needs. While there was a risk of someone robbing the bank, it was minimal as the person had to physically be at the bank to rob it.

Now, with the internet, you don't have to physically be there – you could physically be anywhere in the world and try to get funds out of the bank. The risk profile was expanded considerably due to anyone with an internet connection being able to now be a customer, or worse, do something nefarious.

The risk here is that billions of people could expose that weakness on the public-facing website. While there may be a CVSS 10.0 vulnerability on that internal website sitting behind two firewalls, it is less risky than say a CVSS 7.0 vulnerability sitting on a public server where 30 billion devices can access it.

GV.RM-07

Strategic opportunities (that is, positive risks) are characterized and are included in organization cybersecurity risk discussions.

Many of us think of cyber risk in the negative. For instance, let's say a new vulnerability was identified and you have two systems that are susceptible to it. This is a negative risk. However, there are positive risks too and these come in the form of risk reduction measures or opportunities to obtain countermeasures to correct identified risks.

You should perform an analysis of negative and positive risks. This will assist conversations with staff members and the ELT about how you are minimizing negative risks in the environment. Positive risk can be accomplished by reducing the risks associated with the asset, which can align with the overall business goals and objectives.

You've identified that you aren't minimizing your vulnerabilities due to a lack of a vulnerability identification system. This should prompt you to acquire an application to perform these scans. The acquisition of the mitigating control is a positive. You have now identified a way to gather vulnerability information and developed a strategy for how you want to minimize those vulnerabilities in the environment. A positive would be that you remediated, say, 10 vulnerabilities in the course of a few short weeks.

NIST goes on to describe positive risks as realize, share, enhance, and accept, whereas negative risk responses include mitigate, accept, avoid, and transfer. A positive risk is a strength or opportunity to perform risk reduction in the environment. Positive risks, along with negative ones, should also go into the risk register for tracking purposes.

Reevaluating your cyber risk posture is important. Do this periodically to ensure that you're on the right track. This should include how you evaluate risk tolerance and who is responsible for accepting the risk.

Next, we'll look at C-SCRM. This is important for many reasons, as you will see in the next section.

C-SCRM (GV.SC)

If you pay attention to cybersecurity news, you'll have noticed that plenty of cyber risk exists in supply chain management. Third-party software and services are easy targets for organizations as it is still an uncommon practice to explore the cyber risk of vendors. However, software developed by **SolarWinds**, along with many open source tools such as PyTorch, are susceptible to these types of attacks and we should stay focused on this effort.

As a cyber professional, it is your responsibility to ensure that IT resources that you don't or can't control are at least vetted. This vetting process will highlight the vendor's cyber posture and **BCP/DR strategy** and will help you gain a better understanding of how the software that you use was developed.

GV.SC-01

A C-SCRM program and its strategy, objectives, policies, and processes are established and agreed to by organizational stakeholders.

This would be the time to assess how you evaluate third-party vendors if a program exists. This assessment will bring about what the program currently looks like and how it should be molded for future engagements with those third parties and others you intend to do business with.

This strategy should include how you want to vet third parties to ensure that they are meeting, or exceeding, your cyber posture expectations. If you decide that you want to enter into a contract with the vendor, have a plan for how you want to understand their cyber posture. Whether or not you want to do questionnaires such as the **SIG Lite** or **COBIT** or questionnaires that are closely aligned with your cyber framework, such as the NIST CSF or ISO 27001, you will need to choose one for the vetting process.

Many organizations travel to the facility where the vendor will be hosting the software so that the organization has a better understanding of their posture. This is the best yet most expensive route as it could mean sending one or more employees to the vendors' site to perform the assessment.

Having policies and standards in place ensures that others in the organization follow your lead when it comes to better understanding their cyber posture. The last thing you want to have happen is the IT department performing the vetting process while the finance department just accepts the vendors' terms and conditions without asking what their security posture is.

Many cloud-based vendors, such as Microsoft and Amazon, post their cyber certification certificates, such as ISO 27001, on their websites. This is to allow those who may want to go into a contract with the vendor to better understand what the posture looks like. This can alleviate the need to assess as the documents are there for you to review. Large cloud-based suppliers do not, and will not, fill out a questionnaire like smaller vendors will, so be picky as to who you do business with.

A third-party risk management committee should also be created. This committee's responsibility is to review enterprise risk imposed by your vendors. When developing the committee, include those from across the organization, not just IT. This committee will review all new vendors coming into the organization, along with current vendors you perform business with.

GV.SC-02

Cybersecurity roles and responsibilities for suppliers, customers, and partners are established, communicated, and coordinated internally and externally.

Roles and responsibilities detail who is responsible for what when it comes to a particular program. In this instance, we should create a **responsible, accountable, consulted, and informed (RACI)** chart with all those involved in the C-SCRM program.

In *GV.SC-01*, we briefly touched on creating a risk management committee that's responsible for third-party risk management. This committee shall have a chair or someone responsible for managing the program and those responsible for all other aspects of the program. This committee shall also have a sponsor from the ELT to ensure that this committee receives the backing and oversight it needs to perform effectively.

This RACI chart could have the chairperson be accountable for all aspects of the risk management program, whereas other departments may be responsible for vetting out the questionnaire that pertains to them directly. Each department should be responsible for reviewing the questionnaire and consulted to ensure that the answers to the questions are within risk thresholds, while those outside of the committee could just be informed of things once the vetting process has been completed.

Also, ensure that these processes are documented so that others know what to do when they're bringing in a new vendor. As mentioned previously, it does no one any good if a department goes off and brings in a new vendor without asking them how they intend to protect your organization from theft or loss of information.

Lastly, there should be a mechanism to allow other departments to pick already vetted third parties that the organization can do business with. Whether this goes into an enterprise risk dashboard or is a simple list of vendors to choose from, there should be a way for those in the organization to pick a vendor and have criteria for why that vendor can be chosen.

For example, maybe you have vetted a financial company to do business with. This financial company was chosen to provide them with sensitive banking information of all your employees for retirement purposes. However, that financial company has now requested that they place a server in your network for bulk file transfers. While you may have vetted this financial company only for transferring sensitive data, it is a new risk to have them place a file server in your network and allow them to manage it.

This would require another stream of work as you now have a vendor that can remotely administer a system within your environment. The same goes for other vendors – if you or another department decide that it is time to procure a different set of products and services, this would require yet another assessment of their security posture.

GV.SC-03

C-SCRM is integrated into cybersecurity and enterprise risk management, risk assessment, and improvement processes.

Much like what we did previously when we created the enterprise risk management program and risk registers, we must do the same thing with our vendors. During the vetting process, there are bound to be questions that weren't answered the way we liked or we have concerns about lacking controls. If you decide that you still want to perform business transactions with that vendor, the cyber-related risks should be placed into a risk register.

These risks, once identified, should be worked on so that they can be completed by both your organization and the vendor. This is a shared responsibility between the two companies as there is a shared interest in ensuring that the products and services being delivered are as secure as possible.

There should also be an escalation path when something doesn't go as planned. During the vetting process, ensure that you're asking questions about disaster recovery and business continuity. The products and services that your organization consumes can become critical to your organization. You'll want to ensure that the vendor is abiding by their **service-level agreements** (SLAs) and providing the services you requested promptly.

For example, let's say you've vetted out another financial organization to do payroll for your employees. Have you asked the right questions about whether or not they can perform their duties when needed? What if their systems were attacked by malware and couldn't pay your employees because their systems were out of commission? Do you or your organization have a backup plan in the event of a missed paycheck?

Ensure that when you develop your cyber strategy, it includes third-party risk management. They are an extension of your organization and should be held accountable when something doesn't go as planned. If the vendor falls outside of compliance with your policies, follow up with them to ensure that they comply with your organization's cyber risk tolerance.

GV.SC-04

Suppliers are known and prioritized by criticality.

When you're identifying your third-party suppliers, ensure that they have a criticality label associated with them. This is to ensure that, during a crisis, you know which ones are of most importance to your organization. That's not to say that all of your vendors are important – some may just be more important than others.

For example, the financial institution that's paying your employees is highly critical compared to the office supply company that supplies your pens and pencils. Both of them have their importance, just one is more critical than the other.

GV.SC-05

Requirements to address cybersecurity risks in supply chains are established, prioritized, and integrated into contracts and other types of agreements with suppliers and other relevant third parties.

There should be a mechanism in place to hold a third party accountable if they fall out of compliance with your policies and standards. Typically, this mechanism is done through terms and conditions or a master agreement contract. In these documents, it should be spelled out that if you decide to sign up for a 3-year service, for example, the vendor is required to maintain a certain level of compliance during that time. This means they cannot be great on day one and then slack off for the rest of the contract.

It should be noted that this includes not only the company but also their employees. Ask whether or not they perform background checks on their employees. Not all programs require this, but many do. Check how they monitor their employees for theft or insider threats of sensitive information.

If software is being developed, require the vendor to provide a **software bill of materials (SBOM)**. This SBOM should detail the types of software used, the programming languages, how they vetted their software for bugs and vulnerabilities, and more. You can even require that the vendor provide evidence that they're scanning their systems for vulnerabilities and how they plan to remediate them. If the software is changed at any time, the SBOM should be updated to reflect that and sent to you and your organization.

Don't develop a sense of comfort that the software was made by the vendor and is free from bugs or vulnerabilities. Often, software is outsourced to another company for development purposes. Ensure that you're scanning the software and remediating those vulnerabilities promptly. This may mean having to go back to the vendor to determine the level of risk of having an unpatched piece of software running in either your or the vendor's environment.

The contracts should also provide a clause that stipulates that if the organization determines that the vendor has fallen out of compliance, or has not fulfilled their obligations per their SLAs, then you can terminate the contract. Your information should be important and it should not be left up to a third party to determine how you plan to secure the environment. Remember, it's your name that will be on the paper when an event occurs, not the vendors'.

GV.SC-06

Planning and due diligence are performed to reduce risks before a formal supplier or other third-party relationship is entered.

Previously, we brought up SIG Lite, a questionnaire produced by **Shared Assessments**. This questionnaire asks a series of questions that are meant to promote or highlight a vendor's cyber posture and also better understand where their shortcomings are. COBIT is another framework that can be used to ask questions about a vendor's cyber risk management program. There are hundreds of predefined questionnaires available for you to use, though you can create your own questionnaire. The point is that you want to vet the vendor's cybersecurity program and see how it aligns with yours.

These questionnaires don't necessarily have to be a one-and-done thing either – they could be sent out yearly to ensure that the vendor is maintaining their posture. If the third party utilizes a CSP to host their platform, assess that CSP too. These are known as N^{th} suppliers. They are often called 4th parties as your chosen vendor also has vendors they work with.

GV.SC-07

The risks posed by a supplier, their products and services, and other third parties are understood, recorded, prioritized, assessed, responded to, and monitored throughout the relationship.

Once everything is said and done, and you have collected the questionnaires and the evidence, it is time to review the material. This review should align the answers and evidence provided against the organization's policies and standards. If, for some reason during the review process, you determine that the vendor has a lot of opportunities for improvement, it may be time to discuss how you want to engage that vendor moving forward. Or if the risk is too high, you can cancel the contract altogether.

If you decide to move forward, and the cybersecurity posture is lacking, you may want to write that there needs to be an annual review process in the contract. This review process should take into account how the vendor is remediating the lacking controls in their environment. If you determine that the vendor isn't making progress in remediating the findings, then it may be time to cancel the contract.

You and your vendor management committee will also need to consider what would happen if that service experienced an outage – or worse, you had to cancel the contract due to lacking controls. How would your organization function without said service being in place? Could it survive for an hour, day, or week without having that service available? These are all questions to consider when you're reviewing the importance of the vendor and utilizing their tools.

GV.SC-08

Relevant suppliers and other third parties are included in incident planning,
response, and recovery activities.

We've touched on this a little bit already, but how would you communicate an issue with your supplier? How would the vendor communicate an issue with your organization? These two questions are the premise of this objective. Communication is key when an incident occurs and seconds count during an issue.

Your incident response and recovery plans should have this information in place to communicate an issue when it arises. Building a criticality matrix of your suppliers will also be key during an outage. You must understand the criticality of the vendor and what they supply to your organization. On the flip side, you must also understand the products and services that your organization produces for your customers.

If the vendor were to experience an outage due to their CSP having an issue, how does that get communicated to your organization? How do you respond when there is such an issue? Can you failover to another system while the outage is underway? What are the procedures that you and the third-party vendor must perform to bring that service back up and running again?

This should all be documented in a runbook that both parties have agreed to. If not a runbook, at least have a contact email or phone number for the vendor so that you can contact them in the event of an outage or cyber-related incident. If the vendor is responsible for maintaining the service and it goes down, do they have a crisis communication plan in place to discuss with their stakeholders?

You can also include third-party vendors in your tabletop exercises. If you have a managed security provider that maintains your cybersecurity operations, perform tabletop exercises with them to understand how both sides will react during an incident. You need to practice and build muscle memory for what to do and how to do it during an incident.

GV.SC-09

Supply chain security practices are integrated into cybersecurity and enterprise
risk management programs, and their performance is monitored throughout the
technology product and service life cycle.

The vendor management committee should have a direct line to the ELT, or at least to their committee sponsor. This will allow you to communicate various degrees of cyber risk that were presented by your third-party vendors to the leadership team. This reporting shall also include how they are maintaining the software and/or hardware that your organization uses.

Ensure that the third party is performing maintenance on their equipment and software regularly. This will require a review of both your organization's and the vendor's policy documents to determine whether they align with your expectations. Any discrepancies should be placed into a risk register and then promoted to the enterprise risk register if the risk is high enough to cause concern in the organization.

GV.SC-10

C-SCRM plans include provisions for activities that occur after the conclusion of a partnership or service agreement.

You should have processes in place to remove hardware and software from a former employee's possession when they are ready to leave the company. You should also have similar policies and standards in place for when a vendor contract is up and you don't plan on renewing it.

This should include the removal of software from your organization's systems and the removal of any hardware that might have been placed in the environment. If an implementation plan was created when the contract was first signed, you should be able to work that document in reverse when removing their components from your environment.

Vendor lock-in can be of concern too. Many third parties utilize their own proprietary format for storing information. This can make it extremely difficult for you to transfer your data from one provider to another. Ensure that the contract stipulates that if you intend to use this data in another place, the data can be transferred in a readable format.

Lastly, ensure that any user accounts that were created for the vendor's use are also removed from the systems. This will prevent them from logging into your systems later or leaving a large hole in your infrastructure since you'll have stale user accounts in your environment.

C-SCRM will be crucial to your cybersecurity program. When working with your third parties, remember that they are an extension of your cyber program. They may hold onto sensitive information or control parts or all of your infrastructure. Treat them as you would with any other employee on your staff. The next section will talk about roles and responsibilities between you, your staff, the ELT, and third-party vendors.

Roles, responsibilities, and authorities (GV.RR)

This family of controls is centered around integrating cybersecurity into the roles and responsibilities of your employees. From when the employee was first hired in, to on-the-job responsibilities, or when the employee decides to leave the organization, it's embedded in everything the employee does. This will all need to be documented and approved by management as they too will have to play an active role in how the program evolves and adapts to new threats.

GV.RR-01

Organizational leadership is responsible and accountable for cybersecurity risk and fosters a culture that is risk-aware, ethical, and continually improving.

First and foremost, a cybersecurity charter should be written to ensure that the responsibilities of the program are understood. This charter should include not only the responsibilities of the program and department but also the roles of those who make up the program. These roles should be determined, understood, and approved by the ELT.

A RACI chart should be developed to better understand the roles and responsibilities of those who make up the department. It should also encompass those that are a part of the risk management committee. This committee should provide oversight of the program and risk management decisions for how to handle identified risks. It can be made up of peers, the ELT, or other co-workers within the organization. You may also want to bring in outside counsel if you need to lean on those outside of the organization.

The RACI chart and cybersecurity charter should then be reviewed and approved by the ELT and those who make up the risk committee. The risk committee is responsible for all risks associated with the organization, both internal and external. They will be the ones who make the decisions on how to handle risk, but most importantly, they will have the backing of the ELT to ensure that it gets done appropriately.

GV.RR-02

Roles, responsibilities, and authorities related to cybersecurity risk management are established, communicated, understood, and enforced.

This control objective is similar to *GV.RR-01* in that everything is documented and approved by management. The cybersecurity charter and RACI charts will play a significant role in ensuring that risk management is reviewed and approved by the risk management committee.

In addition to these documents, there will also be the need for policies and standards to be written. These policies will be used to enforce the use of the committee and direct those outside of the committee to follow the procedures when bringing in new vendors. These policies will also have a direct impact on personnel management as you start to engrain a cybersecurity culture in the organization.

You'll also want to ensure that you're gathering meaningful information or metrics for the department so that you can show the progress that's being made. This will be important to understand as you mature the program and get additional funding for projects or deliverables that your department wants to deploy to the organization.

GV.RR-03

Adequate resources are allocated commensurate with the cybersecurity risk strategy, roles, responsibilities, and policies.

The metrics that you have developed to measure your cybersecurity program are only part of what you need to report on. Metrics regarding personnel performance and resource allocation are also of concern. You'll want to ensure that you have enough resources to tackle the challenges that you face as a leader of the cybersecurity program.

You'll also want to ensure that your personnel have the right skills to perform the jobs that they are required to do. You'll want to have your personnel trained in the products and services that are used within the environment. Again, this should all be backed up through policies and standards.

Project planning can also be a source of information. This will draw out resource constraints, if there are any, and help you realize where the sore spots are in your program. With these metrics in mind, it will help you when you go to the ELT to ask for additional resources to maintain your program.

GV.RR-04

Cybersecurity is included in HR practices.

We touched on this one briefly, but you will want to engrain cybersecurity practices in your HR procedures. You will want to ensure that cybersecurity training is embedded into their onboarding process, IT resources or systems rights are applied appropriately, and that HR is conducting background checks for the newly hired employee.

Work with your HR team to ensure that cybersecurity is in the onboarding process. Hit the employee hard (not literally) with training when they're first hired into the company. Have a robust phishing program to reinforce the need for cybersecurity training and gather metrics to ensure that the program is working as intended.

Also, train your HR staff on the importance of offboarding an employee appropriately. You may want to have HR provide **non-disclosure agreements** (**NDAs**) so that they don't disclose what the employee was working on or provide sensitive material to their new company. You may also want to ensure that whoever is receiving the employee equipment does so and that you receive all the equipment back. In addition, you will want to ensure that the employee returns all documents to the company. This is to prevent information leakage and gives the cybersecurity department better control over the information being created.

Depicting roles and responsibilities is important for your program. Understanding who will be doing what during an incident or even during the day-to-day operations can help when you're trying to determine who's responsible. This will all need to be documented and backed up by policy, something we'll discuss in the next section.

Policy (GV.PO)

Chapter 10 will be dedicated entirely to policy life cycle management, but this section will give you a glimpse into what that chapter entails. You'll want to create an entirely new program around policy creation, approval, and annual reviews of the documents. This is not a *set-it-and-forget-it* type of program – it will take dedicated resources to ensure that the program runs appropriately.

GV.PO-01

Policy for managing cybersecurity risks is established based on organizational context, cybersecurity strategy, and priorities and is communicated and enforced.

As mentioned previously, you'll want to create an entirely new program around policy life cycle management. This program will ensure that policy documents are being developed, approved by management, and reviewed annually to ensure that the documents are kept up to date.

You'll also want to ensure that the policy documents, once approved by the committee, are reviewed and signed off on by organizational personnel. This will provide teeth for when an employee states that they were unaware of the policies that are already in place.

A program committee should also be created for the review process of the documents. This committee will be responsible for reviewing and approving policy documents before they're signed off by a member of the ELT or a committee sponsor.

GV.PO-02

Policy for managing cybersecurity risks is reviewed, updated, communicated, and enforced to reflect changes in requirements, threats, technology, and organizational mission.

The review process of policy management is just as important as creating the policy. Policy management should encompass not only creating the policy but also reviewing it and providing updates to the policy if necessary.

For example, in 2014, several organizations were affected by **Heartbleed** [4], which affected legacy versions of SSL and TLS. Maybe you had an encryption standard that stated that you were able to use SSL version 3.0 and TLS versions 1.0 and 1.1. Well, once the Heartbleed vulnerability was released, those were considered insecure.

If your standard wasn't updated, then that meant that it was still acceptable to use legacy versions of SSL and TLS in your environment. Without adequate review and control over your policy documentation, these could still be a standard way of configuring encryption for your web servers.

Ensure that you're updating your policy documents regularly. Many regulatory compliance requirements state that you should review these documents at least annually, if not sooner. This is to ensure that the documents are kept up-to-date and that newer protocols are being standardized within the environment.

This is just scratching the surface of what entails a robust policy life cycle management program. We will discuss this in more detail in later chapters, but it's important to realize that everything that you do should also be documented and reviewed annually or bi-annually. This documentation will play into how governance is handled, something we'll discuss in the next section.

Oversight (GV.OV)

Governance oversight deals with reviewing the overall cybersecurity and governance programs. Here, we'll review **key performance indicators** (**KPIs**) or key metrics that are used to gauge the progress of the program and ensure that it's on track to meet expectations. These indicators are then used to inform and update the program to ensure that it's working effectively.

GV.OV-01

Cybersecurity risk management strategy outcomes are reviewed to inform and adjust strategy and direction.

Throughout this chapter, we've discussed the need to collect metrics for how well the program is working. It's in this control family that we review those metrics to ensure that the program is working as intended. Metrics will also promote the need for additional resources, if required, and also show where the program is lacking.

Where the program may be lacking, we'll look for efficiencies to improve that part of the program. We could introduce more resources or possibly automation into the mix to improve the process. However, without metrics or KPIs, we may not know where the efficiencies or deficiencies reside. We need to have results in hand to know how well the program runs.

GV.OV-02

The cybersecurity risk management strategy is reviewed and adjusted to ensure coverage of organizational requirements and risks.

This may be the time to perform an assessment, either by yourself or via a third party. This will assist you in knowing where your deficiencies are and where you need to improve. Where improvements are needed, readjust your cybersecurity strategy to ensure it's meeting organizational goals and requirements.

This will also require you and your team to run through an after-action review or lessons learned. This is performed at the end of every incident so that you can discover where your shortcomings are and how to overcome them. This will allow you to improve your overall cybersecurity strategy by reviewing what wasn't working and where you have opportunities for improvements.

Maybe you don't have the right documentation written for a particular process. Maybe you need to develop a procedure to work through a particular cyber-related incident. These scenarios are reviewed during the after-action review process to ensure that you can be efficient in rectifying a situation.

GV.OV-03

Organizational cybersecurity risk management performance is measured and reviewed for any adjustments that are needed.

This last control in the oversight family pulls all of this together. Again, pull and review KPIs or metrics for how well the program is running. Ensure that deficiencies are reviewed and prioritized for improvement. Collect these metrics and share them with senior leaders to ensure that the program is aligned with business goals and objectives.

Run tabletop exercises or utilize after-action reviews (why not do both?) to uncover where the program is lacking and align it for improvement. Build policy documents and have them reviewed to ensure that they also align with business objectives. Remember, without oversight and being able to back the ELT, the program will not go in the right direction, or at least the direction that you were hoping for.

Summary

There is a lot to the Govern function. First, we learned that we must ensure that our cybersecurity program portrays the right message to those in the ELT and that we align our program to those initiatives. We must ensure that we review the company's mission and vision statements, along with their business objectives, so that we know what those objectives are. Once understood, we can align our program with those objectives.

We also learned that we need to build KPIs or metrics around how the program is running. This will highlight what's working and what areas need improvement. Share these with the ELT or executive sponsor of your committees so that they're in the know for how well the program is running.

Creating charters with associated RACI charts is important so that people understand what's expected of them. These charters are then used to guide the various programs that will need to be developed to support your overall cybersecurity program. Cybersecurity is just the catalyst for change in the organization. This change will bring about more programs that will need to be developed to sustain the cybersecurity program overall.

Policy and risk management are two of the many programs that will be created to sustain cybersecurity within the organization. This change will affect several departments within the company. From HR to finance, you will need to work closely with these departments and many others to ensure that the program runs smoothly and efficiently.

These changes will also affect how you work with third-party vendors. The program will need to ensure that the products and services that are procured are running as intended within their given SLAs. Additional scrutiny will need to be performed when evaluating the security posture of the vendor. Send out questionnaires to these vendors and request evidence that they're following the guidelines that they set out to do. Hold them accountable when they aren't meeting your expectations.

Lastly, update your contract language with the third-party vendor so that they know what's expected of them. This language will ensure that if they do fall out of compliance with your policies and standards, then you have the right to either work with the vendor to bring them back into compliance or terminate the contract altogether. Remember, it isn't their name that will be in the paper when there's an incident; your company's name will be there too.

In the next chapter, we'll discuss the Identify function and the need to record everything in your environment. This includes recording both known and unknown devices and placing them in a configuration management database.

References

1. `https://nvlpubs.nist.gov/nistpubs/CSWP/NIST.CSWP.29.pdf`

2. `https://www.upguard.com/blog/the-cost-of-downtime-at-the-worlds-biggest-online-retailer`

3. `https://nvlpubs.nist.gov/nistpubs/fips/nist.fips.199.pdf`

4. `https://owasp.org/www-community/vulnerabilities/Heartbleed_Bug`

4
Identify

In the previous chapter, we learned about the *Govern* function and its importance for evaluating and communicating risk throughout the organization. We also highlighted the importance of having an enterprise risk register, cybersecurity supply chain risk management, and oversight. Gathering metrics around your cybersecurity program will not only highlight where you need resources but also evangelize those positive risks.

The need to identify and remove risk from your environment is critical to the success of your program. Once a risk has been identified, you need a place to track it. A risk register can be used to track cyber risk in your organization. I recommend having a risk register per scoped environment. This keeps the register manageable while quickly finding the risk. Once you have developed individual risk registers, generate an enterprise risk register or risk management dashboard. This dashboard will provide a way of highlighting the critical risks discovered within the environment and allow you and your team to remediate those risks effectively.

In this chapter, we will discuss the *Identify* function. The *Identify* function is unique because it requires you to keep track of all your software and hardware assets in the organization. In addition to identifying your assets, you must keep an accurate record of everything in your environment, perform risk assessments, and improve upon those processes. You cannot protect what you cannot see. If you do not keep accurate counts for known and unknown devices, how will you know what is and is not in your environment?

In this chapter, we will cover the following:

- Asset management
- Risk assessment
- Improvement

Let us jump right in!

Asset management (ID.AM)

Reiterating what I mentioned previously, you cannot protect what you cannot see. To effectively protect your organization, you must have a grasp on what is in your environment. This requires that you know the various types of hardware and software that are connected to the network and, more importantly, how you go about protecting those assets.

Some of this will also set you up for success in later chapters. As we begin to lay the foundation of asset management, we will categorize and prioritize these assets, too. This will help in incident response or disaster recovery scenarios as you will know what is of most importance to the organization.

ID.AM-01

"Inventories of hardware managed by the organization are maintained."

This one can sometimes be easier said than done. We must take a holistic view of the environment and understand what is connected to it. We often think about just the hardware or the software, but what about the firmware that programs the hardware? This should be inventoried as well to ensure that it, too, is being updated like the rest of the environment. We also need to inventory what is unknown to the network. For example, cybersecurity professionals make a big fuss about rogue access points being plugged into the network, and for good reason. We do not want insecure access points being plugged into the network, allowing anyone with a Wi-Fi card the ability to connect. This needs to be tracked and inventoried, too.

The best way of capturing this information is by using a **configuration management database** (**CMDB**). A CMDB is used to capture all the information needed to keep track of hardware that is within the environment. In the CMDB, you will want to capture the IP address, hostname, MAC address, location, and who is responsible for maintaining the device. You must also capture the amount of hard drive space or how much RAM is installed. You should capture the CPU make, model, speed, and system architecture. For network equipment, maybe you will want to know the circuit number or management IP of the device.

You will also want to capture all your laptops and desktops. These are just as important as the servers installed at the organization. This will come in handy if a laptop were ever lost or stolen. That way, you can know the device's configuration and whether the hard drive was encrypted.

Capturing rogue devices is important, too. You will want to know what is connected to the network at any given time. Without capturing rogue devices, you will not know where they are located, what their IP address is, or what type of service the device is trying to provide. It may sound counterintuitive; however, capturing this information will provide valuable information when trying to track down who the owner of the device is.

This will need to be performed on a continual basis to ensure that you have the most accurate and updated information. If you do not have the ability to constantly monitor the environment, at least perform an audit every 6 months. Devices should not change too often and you will want to ensure that the CMDB is kept up to date whenever there is a change in the environment.

ID.AM-02

"Inventories of software, services, and systems managed by the organization are maintained."

Much like we saw in ID.AM-01, we must take inventory of the software and services the organization maintains. Your CMDB should have placeholders for the various types of software that are being used. When taking inventory, be sure to include the manufacturer of the software, its version, and the various components of the software.

When capturing the software being used, ensure that there is a **software bill of materials** (**SBOM**) that goes with it. This will tell you the components being used in the software itself. Maybe it is a Java-based web application that runs on Apache Tomcat. It could be a WordPress application that is running PHP and JavaScript. How would you know if you were not capturing that information?

As we will see in the risk assessment portion of *Identify*, you must also scan the environment for vulnerabilities. When trying to remediate those appropriately, you will want to know the various types of software development packages being used so that you can update them.

This goes for the services, not just the software development stack. When setting up a Linux server to handle DNS or DHCP, you must ensure that information is also captured in the CMDB. This will assist in pinpointing any potential issues that may arise due to a vulnerability. For example, previous versions of BIND DNS have been susceptible to vulnerabilities. You will want to ensure that BIND's version numbers are also in the CMDB for traceability purposes.

Like the previous control, you will have to constantly monitor your environment for additions or changes. The **Simple Network Monitoring Protocol** (**SNMP**) can be leveraged for this. SNMP is a monitoring protocol used to monitor components of a system and it can also tell you the installed software, how much hard drive space you have left on a disk, and the IP addresses it may use, among other things. SNMP is a rather old protocol; however, it can capture information and place it into some flat file or database. Use SNMP in addition to your CMDB to ensure that it is constantly updated.

ID.AM-03

"Representations of the organization's authorized network communication and internal and external network data flows are maintained."

Creating network flow diagrams is also an important part of capturing required information about our network. The network diagram should show the systems, network equipment, IDSs/IPSs, firewalls, and other sensors being used to capture threat information of the network. This will not only provide valuable information to your teams in relation to how the network is set up but this information will also be handy in the event of a threat actor trying to gain access to the network.

Network flow diagrams depict how the network was constructed. They also show you where the systems are installed and in which part of the network. Maybe you have multiple firewall "zones" to protect the systems and services. These zones should also be depicted to show where the placement is for that system. The network should show the locations and the types of sensors are being used to show where you are gathering sensitive cybersecurity information accurately.

Your diagrams should also show incoming and outgoing network flows for systems outside the network. For example, you might use a **cloud service provider** (**CSP**) to run a server or utilize a **Software-as-a-Service** (**SaaS**) provider to store **personally identifiable information** (**PII**). Network flow diagrams should also show how that information is going from your network to theirs. *Figure 4.1* depicts a simple network flow diagram:

Figure 4.1 – Network flow diagram

A user is connected to a web server located in AWS. This web server is connected to a database that is being backed up to an S3 bucket. The diagrams can be more complicated than this, but they should show how communication from one user or component to another is handled.

We know that the **Transmission Control Protocol** (**TCP**), during its communication streams, is bi-directional. However, it is important to note that when creating the network flow diagram, the arrows are in the direction from which the communication was initiated. This is also an important distinction as you want to know where the communication is initiated to apply firewall rules correctly.

ID.AM-04

"Inventories of services provided by suppliers are maintained."

The size and scope of the environment will dictate the size of your CMDB. It could contain tens, hundreds, or thousands of systems and services being used within your environment. As mentioned previously, it can contain IP addresses, MAC addresses, system owners, and operating system versions, among others. In addition to that, you should collect network and application flow diagrams and place them into the CMDB as well. The CMDB also be used to capture the service provided by suppliers or third-party vendors.

When making your data flow diagrams, think about all the various system components and services a supplier delivers. Do they supply a **Directory-as-a-Service** (**DaaS**), or maybe even SaaS-based multifactor authentication? If these systems and components are housed by a third-party vendor, you should also capture this information in the CMDB. In your CMDB, you may also want a menu for which components are housed internally and which ones are external to your organization. This will bring to light additional risks you may not be considering. For example, if you mark sensitive data as critical with the intention that it should never leave the walls of your buildings but then you see it stored in cloud storage, that is a significant risk.

You will also want to capture any SaaS components installed within your environment. Several SaaS providers will need on-premises systems and services to securely capture and send information to their cloud. This will also need to be inventoried in the CMDB, and network flow diagrams for how they communicate back and forth will need to be created.

ID.AM-05

"Assets are prioritized based on classification, criticality, resources, and impact on the mission."

Inventorying IT resources is a big component of your CMDB. Getting all of the right parameters needed for capturing the information and then placing the correct information into those parameters can be an undertaking. An afterthought that many people have when creating the CMDB is ranking their systems in order of importance. This can be critical for many reasons, especially when considering IT resource importance during an incident.

Use a tiering structure for your IT resources so that you know which resources should come up first in the event of a disaster. You could have hundreds or even thousands of servers in the network without prioritizing them; how would you know their importance? When tiering a system or group of systems, understand how they fit in the environment. This may be a conversation with the **executive leadership team** (**ELT**) and the business unit to understand better what is important to them.

Maybe your payroll or HR systems need to be up and running 24/7 to ensure that people are paid on time or can process a direct deposit change. Maybe you have a supplier that provides mission-critical services to your business, and you must ensure they are constantly up and running. When a disaster hits, you need to know their level of importance to the organization. A tiering structure could look like this:

- **Tier 1 – Mission critical systems**: These systems are required to run for the business to function. A tier 1 system outage will drastically affect how the business functions.

- **Tier 2 – Secondary mission-critical systems**: These systems are dependencies of tier 1 systems, or their components provide critical services to the business.

- **Tier 3 – Systems or system components that do not provide mission-critical services**: This could include systems that could be down for hours or days without impacting the business.

ID.AM-07

"Inventories of data and corresponding metadata for designated data types are maintained."

Other attributes to capture in your CMDB are sensitive data types that could be stored, processed, or transferred from one system to another. This includes information that could be stored in a SaaS provider system or your CSP. Without this information, you would be unable to determine the criticality of the information stored in an IT resource.

Your CMDB should also capture sensitive data types. These include the following:

- PII

- Data privacy laws such as the **California Consumer Privacy Act (CCPA)** or the **General Data Protection Act (GDPR)**

- Credit card information

- Health information

- Government-regulated information such as Controlled Unclassified Information

This could be a checkbox depicting the type or a text field where you can enter this information. You may also need a system or service to detect and automatically determine your environment's various sensitive data types. It is one thing to start from scratch; it is another to have hundreds of thousands of files with varying data types that you must sort through. I recommend getting a service to help automatically determine the data types of the files for you. This will ease the administration of labeling data types of files.

In your CMDB, you should also determine who the data steward is for the information and metadata. This person will be responsible for accurately determining the data types stored on a file server. They will also be the point of contact for understanding the criticality of the information and what it is being used for.

You will also want to understand the flow of sensitive information. This flow of information can be depicted in a diagram for ease of understanding of where the data resides and where it flows. In an incident, this will come in handy when determining where PII is located, and which components may have touched that sensitive information.

ID.AM-08

> *"Systems, hardware, software, services, and data are managed throughout their lifecycles."*

Most, if not all, systems, services, and data should have a lifecycle attached to them. This lifecycle should be put in place to help determine their criticality and whether they are in use. This can be done through the development of policies, standards, and procedures to help with a lifecycle program.

Businesses typically have a lifecycle management policy that states a laptop or server can only be used for a predetermined number of years (3–5 years for most). Once this time frame is up, that IT resource is decommissioned, and a new one is provided. This is to stay up to date with software, firmware, and hardware components that may no longer be supported.

Software is the same thing. Not all software is maintained indefinitely; it, too, has a lifecycle. Microsoft, Apple, and even Linux distributions release new operating systems every few years or so and stop maintaining the old ones. You could miss out on security or software packages if you do not stay current. Maintaining a software and hardware lifecycle is critical to the success of your cybersecurity program.

It goes without saying that information also has a lifecycle. Your organization should have a data or information lifecycle management policy in place to ensure that when data is no longer needed, it is also destroyed. This will help with data leakage, as old or outdated information typically gets less oversight than updated credit card or PII information.

This lifecycle management also includes successfully deleting information when no longer required. Information should be securely wiped from hardware components such as hard drives and thumb drives when no longer needed. This, too, will help prevent data leakage or accidental loss of sensitive information. You should have policies in place that dictate how a component should be wiped or securely deleted files. NIST has created a document to guide how to delete information securely. This document is called *NIST SP 800-88 – Guidelines for Media Sanitization* [1].

A CMDB will become the central hub for your IT program. It should have the ability to track everything for you in one centralized location. The CMDB can be used for more than just tracking systems and services. It can also be leveraged for incident response procedures. In the next section, we will discuss the necessity of having a risk assessment performed on your environment.

Risk assessment (ID.RA)

Risk assessments assist in identifying risk throughout the organization. Risk identifiers can include vulnerabilities, threats, and understanding what the impact is from those identifiers. We must associate identified system risks with our risk register too for tracking and remediation purposes.

ID.RA-01

"Vulnerabilities in assets are identified, validated, and recorded."

You will need a tool to help identify vulnerabilities and risks associated with your IT resources. This tool should be validated by outside third-party firms to ensure that you are receiving accurate and up-to-date information regarding the risks. There are several vulnerability scanners out there to choose from. Some require a fee or subscription, whereas others are free open source tools that you can use.

Pick a vulnerability scanner that will highlight risks associated with your IT resources. Not all scanners are created equal. PCI, for instance, requires that you use an **approved scanning vendor** (**ASV**) when scanning for vulnerabilities. Many scanners offer the ability to install agents on systems, whereas others may just scan your environment for vulnerabilities. The type of service you choose will determine the level of accuracy in highlighting risks.

If you choose to use a scanner (those without agents), ensure that you configure the scanning software to perform authenticated scans. Authenticated scans provide more accurate results than, say, a scanning engine that only scans the outside of a system or service. You will also need to have a policy and procedure in place to remediate those risks in an appropriate manner.

Vulnerability scanners are just one component of a successful risk management program. Gathering threat intelligence is also necessary for understanding your overall risk. For example, the **Cybersecurity and Infrastructure Security Agency** (**CISA**) maintains a list of **known exploited vulnerabilities** (**KEVs**). This list is freely available to subscribers and notifies recipients of new threats that are discovered. With this intelligence, you can make risk-based decisions on which patches or vulnerabilities should be remediated quickly.

You can also hold after-action reviews or lessons-learned activities to help determine whether the current process is working or where improvements should occur. After-action reviews are performed after an event has occurred; this could be an incident or can be performed after a project has been completed. Ensure that policies and procedures are part of the review process to ensure that they, too, are being updated to ensure everything is running smoothly.

ID.RA-02

"Cyber threat intelligence is received from information sharing forums and sources."

As previously mentioned, the CISA KEV catalog is a great resource for receiving threat intelligence information. This information enriches your current risk and vulnerability management programs, but it is not the only resource you can use to obtain this information.

While there are plenty of paid-for threat intelligence services available, there are free ones that you can choose to subscribe to. Several countries, including the US, have **computer emergency readiness teams (CERTs)** providing threat intelligence. US-CERT has a mailing list that can be subscribed to to receive vulnerability information. You and your organization can be part of an **Information Sharing and Analysis Center (ISAC)** or partner with government agencies such as the FBI **Domestic Security Alliance Council (DSAC)** to receive and provide sensitive cyber-related information.

Having vulnerability or threat intelligence information can also provide valuable intel that can be pumped into **security information and event management (SIEM)** or CMDB. This will assist in identifying which systems have the highest risk and what should be remediated as quickly as possible. For example, you have deemed that a system is externally facing, taking credit card information, and has several vulnerabilities that must be remediated. This information can be pulled out of CMDB to help determine the criticality of the system and when it can be updated.

Threat intelligence may also provide **tactics, techniques, and procedures (TTPs)** for how adversaries try to access your system. MITRE has developed the ATT&CK Framework [2], which has 14 different categories for how an attack can occur and the types of controls you can put in place to mitigate them. Click on any of the attack vectors on the website to read a full description of what the attack is and the intent of the attack. It will also provide examples for mitigation and detection of the attack.

ID.RA-03

"Internal and external threats to the organization are identified and recorded."

Now that you have subscribed to a threat intelligence feed or two, you can begin identifying threats in the environment. Once a threat is identified, you must act on it. If it affects your organization, you must record it in a database or a spreadsheet and determine how you want to handle the risk. This can also be placed into the risk register for recording purposes.

Recording vulnerabilities and how you want to handle them can be a metric you use to report on, as well. Metrics based on the threats and vulnerabilities that either impact or do not impact your organization can be helpful when determining effort. For example, Log4j seemed to set the internet ablaze when it was first released. You would have needed a vulnerability management scanning engine to determine whether your organization was susceptible to the Log4j vulnerability attack. If you were vulnerable to it, an entry in the risk register should show the vulnerability type and the affected IT resources. At this point, you can create a project plan for how you want to resolve it.

If you were not susceptible to it, you would also want to capture that fact to show you are performing your due diligence. Auditors or third-party assessors, including your customers and vendors, will want to know whether a particular vulnerability was introduced into your environment and what your response was to the issue. If you show that you are doing nothing about it, this could indicate to your customers that they may want to go elsewhere.

ID.RA-04

"Potential impacts and likelihoods of threats exploiting vulnerabilities are identified and recorded."

When evaluating the criticality of your IT resources, ensure that you understand the criticality of the system. This can be part of the tiering structure that was previously discussed or some other type of identifying factor. Ensure that this is recorded in a centralized platform such as your CMDB.

Work with internal and external stakeholders to understand the likelihood and impact of a threat that affects the organization. Understand how that risk will impact a system or group of systems if impacted by a given threat. This will also help you understand where you may need additional resources to ensure critical systems are patched and vulnerabilities have been remediated.

You should also run tabletop exercises to identify gaps in your response to threats against IT resources. This will help build muscle memory for responding to a given incident when it does arise. This is all meant to improve your response to an identified threat or risk.

A tabletop exercise is a scenario-based exercise where you can run through a series of questions to a group of team members, typically your **incident response** (**IR**) team, to see how they react to a given scenario. For example, you could run a tabletop exercise where your organization is hit by a ransomware attack or experiences an account takeover from a business email compromise. These are typically run once a quarter and are used to build muscle memory for your team. It is also a time to see their reactions and build metrics around mean-time-to-detect and mean-time-to-respond.

ID.RA-05

"Threats, vulnerabilities, likelihoods, and impacts are used to understand inherent risk and inform risk response prioritization."

As you understand the threat and likelihood of risk impacting your systems, you can take this further and perform risk evaluations on the IT resource. Risk evaluations are meant to highlight the risks inherited from an IT resource. Once those have been identified, you can build project plans for remediation.

Perform targeted security assessments against a given IT resource to understand your risks better. The targeted risk assessment can be a set of questions used to understand the security controls implemented on a given system or device. For example, a targeted risk assessment could highlight whether or not an AV application is installed or multifactor authentication is being used. It could help determine whether a firewall protects the environment and the rules for accessing those systems. These controls should be recorded in a targeted risk assessment document or a **systems security plan** (**SSP**).

In the SSP, you should also record all the cybersecurity controls implemented on the device. This will assist you in determining what controls are lacking and where you need improvement. For example, in your SSP, you will record all the security configurations for a given IT resource. If, for instance, you were lacking antimalware software on the system, then that would be a risk that should be recorded into a risk register as part of the SSP. You will then be able to determine your response to a lack of control so that you can plan for additional resources, if needed, to reduce the amount of risk associated with that asset.

ID.RA-06

"Risk responses are chosen, prioritized, planned, tracked, and communicated."

In the *Govern* function, we learned that there are positive and negative risks associated with our cyber program. When responding to negative risk, you must choose how to handle the risks identified for a given IT resource. Negative risk responses include the following:

- **Accept** – You accept the risk and decide to do nothing to mitigate it

- **Mitigate** – You resolve the risk

- **Transfer** – This involves migrating the risk to a third party, which is typically a cyber insurance provider

- **Avoid** – This is typically where you would scrape the project due to a high amount of risk that is too costly to mitigate or due to other business requirements

When accepting the risk, you plan on doing nothing with the risk identified. This means that you accept whatever risks are associated with that IT resource. Mitigating risks is when you reduce the risk to acceptable levels, including implementing a lacking control or reconfiguring a control to ensure that it meets or exceeds risk reduction. Transference of risk is the event that allows you to move the risk to a third-party vendor. Most of the time, this includes using a cyber insurance provider or transferring the hosting of a service to a SaaS provider or CSP. Lastly, avoiding the risk means you intend not to implement the product or resource in the environment regardless of its placement. The risk is just too high.

Whatever you intend, you should also have a project plan or **plan of action and milestone (POA&M)** to perform a particular risk response. The POA&M is meant to help you and the organization handle risk and your intended response. You can place these risks into a risk register that can be discussed with stakeholders to ensure the risk is handled appropriately.

ID.RA-07

"Changes and exceptions are managed, assessed for risk impact, recorded, and tracked."

This control objective will require that you create a new change management process if one does not exist. Change management involves identifying required changes in the environment, determining how to roll back the changes if they are unsuccessful, and communicating those changes to stakeholders.

You need to document the changes being made to a given system. This documentation can be in the form of a change log or another type of format to allow you to track the changes being made to a given system. This change log can also be useful for others to understand how an IT resource was configured and the changes that were made.

The change request should include the risks of making or not making the change, the requirements for making the change, its process, rollbacks, and who is responsible for the change. The change request should also include an approval process to allow others to review the requested change and ensure that the change being made is appropriate.

ID.RA-08

"Process for receiving, analyzing, and responding to vulnerability disclosures are established."

We have discussed ISACs and their importance. Often, an ISAC is only as good as the information it receives. The ISAC must not only send critical risk information to its members but the membership must also share sensitive cyber risk information with the ISAC.

Ensure that you provide critical cyber risk information to your stakeholders, managed service providers, ISACs, or other institutions you conduct business with. This will assist in ensuring that everyone has the most valuable and up-to-date cyber risk information needed to make good decisions on how to handle risk.

If you provide third-party services to your customers, provide them with information about any issues you and your organization may be experiencing to be transparent with those you do business with. This will improve you and your organization and strengthen the relationship between you and your customers.

ID.RA-09

"The authenticity and integrity of hardware and software are assessed prior to acquisition and use."

There are a few different ways you can view the authenticity and integrity of the software and hardware you use. Software developers use cryptographic signatures to ensure that the software being installed on a device is legitimate. Without this signature, any software will not load, preventing someone from installing malicious software onto the device.

Digital signatures are one way of doing this; another way is to run a hashing function against the software. When running a hashing function, you get a unique character value used to determine the integrity of the software. If the hash value were different, that would mean the software has changed and is not the valid software developed by the manufacturer. We can also do this with regular text files. For example, a file that contains `This is a hashed file` would result in a hash value as follows:

```
2c0e7d464573504149e86e8be26a1118b077c7dbee562086900df1943061bae7
```

If we were to change the contents of the file to `This is a hashed file!`, the new results would be as follows:

`10b481d359a851de7efb58b1cc4f0b237014e37be60936ae22da52ac10eb7388`

The contents of the hash values are completely different. The hashing function can be run against files, compiled software, multimedia, or anything on a system.

Be extremely cautious of software developers that do not provide one of the two previous functions. Without a mechanism for checking the validity of software, it could lead to supply chain issues, where the software was manipulated without the developer's knowledge. This could also mean that malware was inserted into the application without anyone's knowledge.

ID.RA-10

"Critical suppliers are assessed prior to acquisition."

As we did with evaluating risk and applying a criticality tier to our IT resources, we should apply the same scrutiny to our suppliers. Depending on the criticality of the vendor's service, this could lead you to want to conduct a risk assessment against the vendor as well.

Third-party vendors are an extension of your network and workforce. They hold onto your sensitive data while providing much-needed services. Because of this, you should be performing evaluations against these suppliers to ensure that their security model reflects your or your business's expectations when safeguarding data. We previously discussed using SIG Lite or COBIT in *Chapter 3* to perform these evaluations. This is a much-needed step in your evaluation of their security controls.

Improvement (ID.IM)

We have put considerable effort into identifying IT resources and performing risk assessments around them. This effort must be placed into a program where continued efforts and improvements are made to ensure that we do not lose sight of identifying and classifying our resources. This next family of controls is meant to ensure that continual improvement occurs to streamline our processes better.

ID.IM-01

"Improvements are identified from evaluations."

While we have discussed in detail how to perform cybersecurity assessments on our vendors and third parties, we should also perform evaluations on ourselves. These evaluations will highlight our deficiencies and build project plans for improvement. Never fear an assessment, as they are meant to help you improve. As discussed in *Chapter 2*, use the Deming cycle to identify areas of improvement and then execute those plans.

Once the assessment has been completed, identify the gaps in your program, build a POA&M for improvement, and make it happen. I would perform these assessments at least every 2 years. However, I would not go beyond that. Do at least one annually if you have the time and can afford to have one performed. Also, automated means for identifying where things need improvements should be set up. Audit your AV, vulnerability management, user access, and data classification. The more you automate, the better you can identify the gaps and improve your program.

ID.AM-02

"Improvements are identified from security tests and exercises, including those done in coordination with suppliers and relevant third parties."

We have not gotten to the *Response* and *Recovery* portions of the framework yet; however, we are beginning to introduce how to future-proof incident response activities. To do this, we can utilize tabletop exercises, penetration testing, and other simulated exercises. While we perform these internally, we should also inquire with our third-party stakeholders to see whether they are willing to participate.

Many organizations outsource some or all of their security engineering and operations. They do this for several reasons; resource constraints and hiring the right people are typically the biggest two. As they are an extension of your team, you must include them in your incident response and recovery plans.

How do you include them? Run an annual tabletop exercise with the provider so that both parties understand what the response should look like. Simulations of attacks are also a great way to not only understand the skill set of your internal staff but also highlight any deficiencies that may come up with your **managed security provider** (**MSP**).

Penetration tests are also a great way to identify gaps in your incident response plans. A fun way to know whether people understand how to respond to an incident is not to tell them that a penetration test is underway. This will help you gauge whether people are paying attention and learning from the exercises.

Build metrics around the mean-time-to-detect and the mean-time-to-respond to a given incident. Know how many vulnerabilities you have in your environment and when these are planned to be remediated. Understand how long it will take to recover from an incident and bring the systems back online. These metrics will assist in the development of new and innovative ways of responding to an incident.

ID.AM-03

"Improvements are identified from execution of operational processes, procedures, and activities."

After-action reviews or lessons-learned activities are a great way of understanding the previous event and whether your response procedures are effective. Conduct them at the end of every incident or project to better understand how the event occurred, why it occurred, and how you and your team responded to it. Much like how we hold tabletop exercises with our third-party vendors, we should hold lessons-learned activities with our trusted third-party vendors, as well.

Lastly, use metrics to determine how to improve your mean time to detect and respond. Maybe you need to improve your incident response plan, communicate differently, or automate more of your response; metrics will help highlight your deficiencies and point you toward improvements in the process.

ID.AM-04

> *"Incident response plans and other cybersecurity plans that affect operations are established, communicated, maintained, and improved."*

We will discuss this more in upcoming chapters; however, you must develop an IR plan. This plan will be crucial for your response to incidents when they arise. Your IR plan should be extensive, including not only the identification of an incident or threat but also how to respond to the threat and how to contact everyone on the team when a threat is discovered. In addition, we need to continually improve the response plan through lessons-learned activities.

We need to strive for tier 3 or tier 4 when it comes to maturity and risk mitigation. We want to ensure that our response to an incident is swift and ultimately easy for our staff members. This will take significant preparation to get your IR team to this level; however, it is important.

Establish policies and standards for how you identify threats and risks, and how you should respond to them. Your CMDB is now your database for the identification and tracking of known and unknown assets in your environment. You can also pump your vulnerability information into a SIEM system to correlate the threats coming in and how you want to respond to them.

Make sure you incorporate lessons-learned activities and update your policies and standards regularly. This will prepare you for future incidents and ultimately reduce your time to detect and respond.

Summary

Building a CMDB, if you do not have one already, will be the focal point for meeting the control objectives in this family. The CMDB shall record all identifying information about the resource; this includes the IP and MAC address of the system, make, model, and who is responsible for it, among others. The information in the CMDB should also include the importance of the resource and whether it is an on-premises, off-premises, or third-party-hosted SaaS offering.

You should also include the software and firmware present on these systems. Both should be updated regularly to ensure the system is free of bugs and vulnerabilities. You should also include rogue devices in your CMDB. Not only will this highlight the need for proper identification of the rogue asset but it will also help you understand what is connected to the network. The CMDB should also hold network flow diagrams, which will come in handy during an incident. The network diagrams should depict what is in the environment, what they communicate with, and even the flow of sensitive information from one point to another. During an incident, you can utilize these diagrams to help you understand the security controls placed on the systems and the types of risks associated with the assets.

Lastly, you should be keeping track of your metrics for the mean times to detect and recover from incidents. Also, keep track of the number of vulnerabilities within the environment and which ones are slated to be remediated. It is important to know and understand this when trying to identify risks within the network.

In the next chapter, we will take a look at the *Protect* function. This function is meant to safeguard your data from those who may want to gain access to it. We will discuss how to leverage encryption to protect your data and detect whether the data was altered in any way.

References

1. *NIST SP 800-88*: `https://csrc.nist.gov/pubs/sp/800/88/r1/final`
2. *MITRE ATT&CK Framework*: `https://attack.mitre.org/`

Protect

We learned a lot about the Identify function in *Chapter 4*. By knowing what is and is not connected to your network, the hardware, software, known devices, and unknown devices, you can build your own database of information. This database, known as a **configuration management database** (**CMDB**), can be paired with other services within your cybersecurity portfolio. This includes enriching information with your vulnerability management system or using it in conjunction with your disaster recovery and incident response plans. Metrics on the number of vulnerabilities, the timeframe from when they were discovered to their remediation, and their risk to the organization are crucial. This collaborative approach enhances your response to an incident. In this chapter, we will cover the Protect function. We will take a look at several different controls, such as how you perform security awareness training, how you protect sensitive information, and how resilient you can make your IT resources. We will continue to build on previous control families by leveraging the same systems that were set up, such as your CMDB.

We will cover the following controls in this chapter:

- Identity Management, Authentication, and Access Control

- Awareness and Training

- Data Security

- Platform Security

- Technology Infrastructure Resilience

Identity Management, Authentication, and Access Control (PR.AA)

In this control family, we will cover how identities are created and managed and how to prove that the identity matches the person using it. Identities do not necessarily have to be those bound to a person; they could also be system-based identities. We must ensure that each identity is unique and that only one entity is assigned to each identity.

PR.AA-01

Identities and credentials for authorized users, services, and hardware are
managed by the organization.

There are several ways to manage your users' credentials. Most organizations utilize a system that provides an identity store. The identity store contains usernames, passwords, groups, and other security-related information. That identity store then works with the **Lightweight Directory Access Protocol** (LDAP) to ensure that it can communicate in a standard way with other downstream systems.

There are several different types of credentials. There are basic credentials that are tied to a user or employee and typically contain just a password or a PIN. There are also shared credentials, those used for a **break-glass** process. These are normally administrative accounts used to log in to the system and perform certain elevated tasks.

A work order typically accompanies the request for a credential. This is to provide a paper trail for those who work in regulated sectors such as CMMC, PCI, and HIPAA. IT will take the request that was initiated by a different department, such as HR, to onboard new users, or remove old users from the identity store.

Each identity should be unique because no two people should have the same username. This will create a conflict if more than one person has the same account. That being said, service accounts should also be unique and tracked for decommissioning purposes. If you continue to use the same service account across multiple systems, you will begin to develop a reliance on that account for everything. Without proper tracking, if something were to happen, such as a need to change the password, you would not know where to change the passwords for the services. This can cause significant security implications.

If you deploy certificates on top of the credentials being used, you will need to revoke those once an employee leaves the company. Cryptographic certificates can, in many cases, be used either as a replacement or in conjunction with a password. Certificate-based authentication is typically tied to an ID card that is provided to the employee upon employment.

Safeguarding user credentials is extremely important, as these identities are capable of logging in to a system. If a credential were lost or stolen, an adversary could log in to your systems without your knowledge. These attacks often lead to system compromise or ransomware.

PR.AA-02

Identities are proofed and bound to credentials based on the context of interactions.

There are plenty of ways to prove an identity. You can ask for proof or verification that a person is who they say they are by requesting a driver's license, social security card, utility bill, or passport. You can also prove your identity physically by verifying a person's government photo ID. These are all different ways of proving someone's identity, but how do you know which is appropriate?

You should always verify a person's identity prior to giving them access to your systems, whether that is through requesting that they come into the office to verify their identity physically or using identification cards. This is a necessary step to ensure the security of your environment. Once proved, IT can then provide the new employee with their credentials for logging in to IT resources.

PR.AA-03

Users, services, and hardware are authenticated.

Now that our employees have credentials, we must authenticate them to a given system or service. There are a few different ways to go about this. We can require just **single-factor authentication** or **multifactor authentication** (**MFA**) to a given device, depending on the risk associated with its tasks. We must also discourage sharing credentials with others, as this defeats the purpose of having unique credentials.

We typically think of authentication as providing a username and password to an IT resource. This is the simplest method of authentication, only requiring the user to provide something they know. But as computers have advanced over the years, so have the techniques for cracking passwords.

Users also experience fatigue in memorizing different passwords. This is due to having access to multiple systems and services, so they use the same password for multiple applications. Threats to third-party services such as LinkedIn and Facebook have led to password dumps of their customers' passwords, often unencrypted. This leads to password-spraying attacks, which use the same passwords found in these dumps against other SaaS-based applications.

This has pushed many online services to use MFA. In addition to something the person knows, they must also have something physical or must verify a characteristic, typically a fingerprint or retina scan. Legacy MFA systems utilized a physical device that had a rotating **one-time password** (**OTP**) or PIN that you had to type in. Modern systems use push notifications to a cell phone in your possession. Physical devices that work with **Fast IDentity Online** (**FIDO**), such as a YubiKey, are also a type of MFA that can be used. FIDO is a newer authentication standard meant to eliminate passwords. It uses public/private key authentication where the **service provider** (**SP**) holds on to your public key and you hold on to the private key.

MFA allows a higher level of proving the identity of the person being authenticated. If someone were to gain access to the password and try to authenticate, they would still not be able to do so due to the necessity of requiring that secondary factor.

MFA is not without its problems, however. **Push fatigue**, where the adversary repeatedly authenticates to the service, which floods the MFA provider, is sending several push notifications in a row in the hopes that they will press the **OK** button. **SIM swapping** is also a threat where the adversary tries to associate the victim's phone number with one in their possession. With these risks, it is still important to use MFA wherever you can to mitigate the risk of a bad password.

PR.AA-04

Identity assertions are protected, conveyed, and verified.

Authentications should be protected from session hijacking, password spraying, and MFA push fatigue and ensure encrypted communication. These are just a few safeguards to consider when choosing a single sign-on provider. There are a few standards that have been developed to help with this, and one is **Security Assertion Markup Language (SAML)** 2.0. SAML 2.0 provides authentication through the **identity provider (IdP)**. The IdP is used to authenticate the user once and then provide a token assertion to the SP.

The communication between the IdP and the SP is protected against attacks, and you can enforce MFA. Another benefit of using a SAML provider is that you can request the user to re-authenticate, making it possible to kill all active sessions in the event of an account takeover.

PR.AA-05

Access permissions, entitlements, and authorizations are defined in a policy, managed, enforced, and reviewed, and incorporate principles of least privilege and separation of duties.

As we grant credentials to our employees, we provide them with access to a given resource. Over time, those credentials can gain what is called **permissions creep**, where an employee who has been transferred to a different department or promoted maintains access to systems they no longer need. Often, when this occurs, the credentials the employee uses maintain their old permissions while gaining new ones. We must look at restricting credentials to only those permissions that employees need to do their daily jobs.

We can also look at **attribute-based authentication control (ABAC)**, which considers much more than just a username and password or the use of MFA. ABAC can consider the location of the user or credential being used, the time of day, what they are trying to access, and their intentions for the access, whether it's to read or write to the document.

We should set aside time for our employees to review access permissions. This will help reduce the number of rights a particular user has, further securing the network. User access reviews should occur at least annually or when a new request is made to change the permissions of a user's account.

PR.AA-06

Physical access to assets is managed, monitored, and enforced commensurate with risk.

Not only do we need to protect the logical side of our IT resources, but we also need to secure the physical side. Data center security should always consider new ways of protecting assets as many logical security configurations can be circumvented. Administrative accounts can be reset using a physical CD inserted into the server, network equipment can be circumvented by setting the registry to a given value, or devices can be reset by pressing a button for 10 seconds.

Many data centers will not only physically secure the environment but also implement several policies and standards for how people are escorted throughout the facility. For example, an employee may want to enter the data center to repair a failed device. We should check to see whether they are even allowed into the data center. Additional background checks are often performed to check whether the person who is trying to enter the facility is trustworthy. We can even decide whether employees can enter the facility by themselves or whether they have to be escorted by a data center official.

We must also establish a reason for an employee entering the facility. This is typically done through a work order requesting access to the facility due to an outage. Even though they may have been granted access to the facility, that does not mean they can go in and out of the data center anytime they want. There must be a reason.

Regardless of whether the employee can gain access to the facility, we still need to verify them. This means requiring the employee to present their employee ID card and sign in on a sheet of paper stating the reason for the visit, as well as presenting the work order number providing them the ability to enter the facility and their reason for visiting.

This goes for guests and vendors as well. Many guests or vendors should not be able to enter the data center without being escorted. If they do not work for your company, you may not want anyone to access the data center without being escorted.

The facility should have several safeguards deployed, including security cameras, guards, and alarm systems. This is to monitor the environment and provide traceability when something goes wrong. We can also have mantraps when entering the server room, requiring one last authorization prior to entering. We can use locked cages and only provide a key to the specific cage in highly secured environments. RFID tags can also be used on the device to trigger alarms if a server were to be removed from the facility.

It is necessary to verify that a person is who they say they are, both physically and virtually. This is to ensure that the correct individuals are performing the intended duties. Security awareness and training is also a critical step when educating your users on the appropriate steps to take when faced with a threat or identified risk. Let's learn how.

Awareness and Training (PR.AT)

The employees at your company are your eyes and ears when it comes to cybersecurity. They are your first line of defense. The employees will often see new threats against your facility before you do. Security awareness and training are not meant just for the cybersecurity professional; it is meant for everyone in the company.

PR.AT-01

Personnel are provided with awareness and training so that they possess the knowledge and skills to perform general tasks with security risks in mind.

There is a difference between security awareness and training. **Security awareness** is meant to provide generalized cybersecurity awareness within the facility. This can mean posting flyers or posters throughout the organization promoting cybersecurity topics. This is meant primarily for those outside of IT.

Security training, on the other hand, is more targeted or focused on cybersecurity topics that provide in-depth knowledge of a particular area. For example, we may be aware of phishing scams or the dangers around the malicious use of QR codes. A focused security topic would be training our firewall administrators on the new firewalls that we just put in place.

Cybersecurity awareness should occur on a regular basis. The sweet spot for this is to do it at least once a month; any longer than that and studies have shown that people lose focus of what they are supposed to do when faced with a risk [1]. Studies show that performing a security awareness program just once a year is as effective as not doing anything at all. This is why performing these programs regularly is beneficial.

Follow up your awareness program with phishing campaigns to reinforce the necessity to use caution when interacting with emails. As phishing is on the rise, you will want to ensure that your employees are being trained on what to do when they encounter a phishing email in their inbox.

As mentioned, focused training is also necessary, but this is typically for IT-related staff. Training can occur at least once a year for your IT and cybersecurity staff. Maybe you need to send them to a class on using firewalls or provide training on a new **intrusion detection system/intrusion prevention system (IDS/IPS)** appliance that was just installed. Focused training is also more expensive than awareness training. Depending on the type of training being requested, it could cost thousands of dollars. This is acceptable for specific employees, not the entire staff.

You can also look at performing presentations for your staff around cybersecurity topics. This can be a fun and cost-effective way of training staff members on security-related topics without the costs of purchasing an awareness program. Be cautious to stay on top of new trends and ways that adversaries attempt to gain access to a network. While this may save you money, it may still be beneficial to use the training provided by a vendor.

PR.AT-02

Individuals in specialized roles are provided with awareness and training so that they possess the knowledge and skills to perform relevant tasks with security risks in mind.

When creating cybersecurity awareness programs, you should be mindful of several specialized roles within the organization. It is important to create a curriculum for those in the executive leadership team, finance, HR, legal, or other departments in the organization, as they face similar yet different challenges when it comes to IT and cybersecurity.

While a generalized cybersecurity awareness program will meet the needs of training your staff, it is also important to understand that these areas have a different focus on the business. The finance department may be concerned with bank or wire transfers, whereas HR members may be concerned about medical records or direct deposit transfers. Having a specialized focus on these areas for the department can be beneficial when focusing on security awareness programs.

These focused areas of training do not have to occur monthly. It is important to remember that this would be on top of your awareness program currently in place. You could have months of generalized awareness and sporadically have a more focused view of risk areas for those departments.

Cybersecurity awareness should also include trusted third parties, vendors, or others with access to your network. Remember, these are considered staff augmentation or an extension of your IT or other departmental staff. They should be required to take the required training just like the rest of your staff. Third-party vendors should also be required to review and sign off on corporate policies and standards, so they know what is and what is not acceptable when using your company's equipment and facilities.

Having covered the need for awareness and training, we now need to look at how we protect data.

Data Security (PR.DS)

Protecting data at rest, in flight, and while it is in use is not the easiest thing to do. Thankfully, however, there are built-in tools that will allow us to protect data at all stages.

PR.DS-01

The confidentiality, integrity, and availability of data-at-rest are protected.

Encryption is the name of the game for this control family. To ensure that we are adequately protecting our information, we must initially encrypt the drives that the data resides on. This is important for many different reasons, but the biggest one is to make sure that if a device were ever lost or stolen, the data could not be retrieved from the hard drive.

It is trivial to take information from an unencrypted hard drive. You can buy a device from any local IT or computer store that will allow you to hook up the drive, through USB, to another computer and read information from it. If the hard drive were encrypted, this would not be the case. In order to decrypt the drive, you would need the key.

Ensure that every drive in your environment is encrypted using full-disk encryption. Microsoft uses a program called **BitLocker**; for Apple devices, there is **FileVault**; and for Linux, there is **LUKS**. Each of these programs will manage the device encryption for you so that you can use the information on the hard drive and then re-encrypt your files once you are done with them. Always use the latest encryption algorithms available to you. This is to prevent someone from performing side-channel attacks against the device and gain access to it without a password.

Also, ensure that you are encrypting removable media such as external hard drives or thumb drives. These devices are just as important to encrypt as the internal hard drives themselves. Loss of these devices will also have a significant impact on your data security if they contain sensitive data such as **intellectual property** (**IP**) or **personally identifiable information** (**PII**) data. Depending on the severity of the data that was lost, you may have to release a statement about it.

PR.DS-02

The confidentiality, integrity, and availability of data-in-transit are protected.

Protecting **data in transit** (information in flight between two or more systems) is just as important as protecting **data at rest** (stored locally on a hard drive or thumb drive) for many reasons. Just as it is trivial to mount an external drive to a computer and read its contents, applications such as Wireshark make it trivial to read unencrypted data in transit, too.

Wireshark has the ability to read packets off of the network wire and determine the protocols being used. We can reconstruct web pages that were accessed to even replay videos or sounds, all from the application. Encrypting data in transit prevents this from happening.

Policies and standards must be written to reflect the need to protect sensitive data. This should include the correct encryption algorithms and bit strengths to use. It should also include which encryption is strictly prohibited. These policy documents are then used to enforce the protection of the data at risk.

Not only should our data in transit be encrypted, but we also need to validate that the message or document was not altered in transit. The only way of doing this is through the use of hashing. As previously discussed, a hash is a cryptographic value that depicts the file at a given time. If the file were ever modified, that hash would change, reflecting that the document is not the same as it originally was.

Digital signatures can also be used to determine the authenticity of the file itself. A digital signature is a cryptographic file that is associated with software or other files that show it was created by a vendor or someone in your organization. It requires the use of a private key to create the signature which is, secured in a protected vault or **hardware security module** (**HSM**).

You should also have mechanisms in place to restrict sensitive data from traveling outside of the facility. You should mark or tag sensitive data in the environment to identify the type of data it is. Then, once the files have been tagged appropriately, apply restrictions to those files to prevent them from being sent across the internet to email or other file transfer protocols such as **SSH File Transfer Protocol** (**SFTP**). This is not to be confused with **File Transfer Protocol Security** (**FTPS**).

Policies should also be created to restrict the use of sensitive information in development or test environments. These environments typically do not have the same security controls as production systems. This leaves sensitive information at risk due to lax cybersecurity controls. Test/development environments should use sanitized information to protect against accidental exposure of data.

PR.DS-10

The confidentiality, integrity, and availability of data-in-use are protected.

Hard drive encryption uses symmetric algorithms to protect data at rest. This symmetric algorithm uses a single password to encrypt and decrypt information located on the drive. When accessing a file, the drive will decrypt the file so it can be used by the application, and then once finished, it will re-encrypt the file back to the drive. This leaves a hole in our security as the file is not protected while it is in use.

We must protect data as soon as possible, especially when it is no longer needed. Modern-day operating systems will remove data from memory as quickly as possible when no longer required. This is to safeguard the data from manipulation prior to discarding it. Review the system and hardware specifications of your devices, including the hard drive encryption applications being used, to safeguard against in-memory attacks.

Not only does this require laptops and desktops to remove this type of information from memory as quickly as possible, but it also applies to network equipment, especially devices that perform **Transport Layer Security** (TLS) offloading. **TLS offloading** is typically used for load-balancing appliances, where the connection must be decrypted for the appliance to decide where to forward traffic. We can also use TLS offloading for data or information discovery to determine the types of files leaving our network.

Regardless of the application, the encryption is broken down to determine what to do with the traffic. This can be a cause of concern if an adversary were to have access to the load-balancing device as they would be able to scrape the memory for not only sensitive information but also any decryption keys that may be used during that time. Be especially careful when performing these transactions to safeguard against sensitive information falling into the wrong hands.

PR.DS-11

Backups of data are created, protected, maintained, and tested.

When determining security controls for a given IT resource, ensure that you are also backing up the resource to meet business expectations. This is to ensure that the data that resides on that system is backed up accordingly. Not all backup strategies are the same; differing systems will have different requirements for performing and testing the backups.

You will need to understand business requirements when discussing backup strategies. Some tier 1 systems may be required to be backed up by the minute to save database transaction logs, whereas tier 2 or 3 systems may be required to be backed up daily. This is all based on the requirements set forth by the business unit.

Performing tests of your backups is just as important as the backup itself. You may be backing up your systems daily, which is great, but what if your backups fail? Did you really have a backup to begin with? Test your backups regularly. Many organizations test their backups quarterly, whereas others may test their backups annually. This is all dependent on the level of risk you are willing to take. If your backup strategy for your databases is to perform them every five minutes, then this should signal that these backups are important and that testing them should occur more often than a tier 3 system that may only be used once a month. That is not to say that the tier 3 system is not important, but that it is less important than the database.

Many backup strategies include the use of both incremental and full backups. Incremental backups are quicker and utilize less storage, which ultimately means lower cost. Full backups are just that, a full backup of the entire system, folder, or file. These take less time to restore; however, they are costly and utilize the most storage. Discuss this with the business units to determine what their expectations are and develop a strategy for what makes the most sense.

It should be of no surprise that backups are filled with sensitive information, whether that is PII, PCI, HIPAA, IP, or other data that may be deemed as sensitive. Much like how we protect data that resides on a hard drive, backups should also be encrypted to protect the data from accidental loss or in the event that it might be stolen. Encrypted backups should be labeled and stored in a secure manner. Organizations will also perform multiple backups or take copies of a single backup and distribute it across multiple geographically distributed data centers. This is to ensure redundancy in the backups so if there were a physical problem with a facility, you could grab a copy of the backup from someplace else.

We must utilize encryption for most if not all of what we do in order to safeguard our data from those who want access to it. Encryption brings a lot of benefits and so does patch and configuration management, which we will learn more about in the next section.

Platform Security (PR.PS)

Much like how we identify our hardware and software, we must also maintain it. Patching is needed to resolve issues with software bugs and vulnerabilities. We should remove old hardware and software from the environment once they have reached their end of life. While we look at the removal of legacy software and systems, we also need to look at our software development life cycle to ensure that it is being maintained appropriately.

PR.PS-01

Configuration management practices are established and applied.

When we first receive an IT resource or go to install software, there are typically system defaults that accompany it. While system defaults provide ease of use when setting up a new device, not changing those defaults will introduce unwanted risks. We must change these defaults prior to placing the systems default into a production setting.

We have all seen and used system defaults before. Ever had to type in `admin` and `password` at an authentication prompt? Used cisco as the username and password when logging in to a network device? These are all examples of system defaults. They are easy to use, guess, and find on the internet. This can lead to unwanted users and adversaries logging in to your network without you knowing.

These, among other system defaults, should be changed prior to moving equipment into production. There are tools available that will help identify which system defaults should be changed. The *Center for Internet Security* has developed hardening benchmarks for a number of different IT resources, such as operating systems, network equipment, firewalls, and databases.

You should also monitor the environment to detect any deviations from the hardened baseline. This is to ensure that configuration drift has not occurred and the resource has stayed within risk tolerance levels. Also, keep a log of all the changes being made. This will require the creation of a **change advisory board** (**CAB**).

This advisory board will be responsible for approving or denying any changes that are made to the system. The CAB will track all changes made to a system for historical purposes and ensure that changes are made at the appropriate time. Often, changes to systems are made without anyone's knowledge and can lead to confusion.

PR.PS-02

Software is maintained, replaced, and removed commensurate with risk.

As mentioned previously, all software follows a life cycle. This life cycle will include many stages; however, software can and always has an end date. Are you still running Windows 2003 in your environment? This software needs to be upgraded in a timely manner in order to install bug fixes and remediate vulnerabilities. This should all be commensurate with the amount of risk you are willing to take.

Develop a patch management life cycle policy that incorporates when patches will be applied. The patch management life cycle policy should also include the patching of software vulnerabilities outside of normal maintenance. This would include high or critical vulnerabilities that should be patched immediately. Your patch management may also have dates and times for when no patching can occur. This is often necessary to ensure that financial systems are online for payroll, for instance.

Have mechanisms in place to restrict what a user can and cannot do on their machine. This can include the removal of administrative rights. This can ease the amount of configuration drift that occurs on a laptop or desktop as the user does not have the capabilities to install their own software.

There are also capabilities for restricting what software can and cannot do on the machine. This occurs when you only want certain applications to run on a system, which is often called the **allow-listing** of applications. The best way of doing this is by reducing a user's rights and only installing the necessary applications that the user needs to perform their job.

PR.PS-03

Hardware is maintained, replaced, and removed commensurate with risk.

Hardware, much like software, has a shelf life that is typically 3–5 years. The length of this replacement cycle can vary depending on the manufacturer; however, note that hardware does not live forever, even if we would like it to. Hardware components go bad, systems may appear to slow down, or you may no longer be able to upgrade the firmware on the device.

When hardware does finally reach its end of life, you must securely discard it. This does not mean throwing it in the trash and getting a new device; it must be disposed of properly. Many hardware manufacturers have created guidelines for how to securely discard a device. There are write-ups for how to remove a hard drive from a system and wipe it so you can no longer retrieve any information from it.

The best way of doing this is to partner with a third-party vendor that specializes in hardware disposal or recycling. These businesses will take your old equipment and discard it appropriately while securely removing any information from a hard drive. Often, the business will provide you with a certificate proving that everything was discarded and that no information resides on the drive. This is important as it creates a paper trail or chain of custody for who had the device last and what was performed.

Again, ensure that you have a scanning mechanism in place to monitor systems within the environment. This can be monitored through the **Simple Network Management Protocol (SNMP)** or other types of monitoring protocols. Your CMDB should also have records of what the device is, the purchase date, its expiration date, and what the latest installed firmware version is. This will help you Make a succession plan for purchasing new equipment or possibly moving the workload to a cloud SP.

PR.PS-04

Log records are generated and made available for continuous monitoring.

As a general rule, if it is connected to your network, then it should log. Many systems log by default, such as operating systems, whereas others require you to activate the logging.

You must develop a plan for how you want to log and where the logs should be stored. Often, systems are stood up with no plans for where the logs should be sent. This could mean that some systems are logging locally whereas others are sending their logs to a SIEM system. You may also run into instances where different systems have different logging retentions. Some could be holding onto logs for a month, some longer, and some may have stopped logging altogether. You will want to perform an assessment to determine your current state of logging.

You will also want to determine how long you want to hold onto the logs. Several regulatory requirements state that you must hold onto the logs for a certain amount of time before offloading them to an offsite storage facility. A general rule of thumb is to have at least 90 days worth of logs on disk, 180 days of logs in a warm storage where you can retrieve the logs when needed, and up to a year's worth offsite.

This should also be stated in your retention policy. Organizations can get themselves into trouble if it is determined that logs are required to determine the outcome of an incident. If you are deleting logs without a policy, it could be seen as tampering with evidence.

There are also several requirements that you should look for in a logging solution. For example, users should be required to log in to a system to view the logs. On top of that, you should require MFA. Administrators should not have the ability to delete logs from a system; only the logging system should have the capability of deleting logs, according to a defined policy. The storage medium being used to store the logs must be encrypted. Lastly, there must be an integrity check to ensure that the log entries being stored have not been tampered with. This is typically performed by creating a hash of the event.

Logs themselves come in many different formats; however, you should look out for certain characteristics. Logs should have a timestamp for when the event occurred. They should each have a sequence number so that you can trace the event. This is also to ensure that there are no lost entries in the log file itself. If it is a network-based device, it should contain both a source and destination IP and possibly a port number. A user account should also accompany the event to trace it back to a given user.

PR.PS-05

Installation and execution of unauthorized software are prevented.

We touched on this previously; however, we must take a least-privileged approach when it comes to the abilities that a user has on a device. In many situations, logging in as a local administrator is unnecessary and can cause instability within systems. Software should be digitally signed and verified to ensure the authenticity of the application being installed.

There are additional ways to protect the installation of software. **Mobile device management** (MDM) can be set up to provide a company or enterprise store where only allowed applications can be installed from. MDM software allows you to control the version of the software as well. This helps when you have an application that only runs a specific version of Java, for example.

PR.PS-06

Secure software development practices are integrated and their performance is monitored throughout the software development life cycle.

If your organization develops software for internal resources, or for external customers, it should have a life cycle associated with it. There are plenty of ways to protect your code during the process and manage how the code is disposed of once it is no longer in use. Let us take a look.

You should digitally sign your code throughout the life cycle to protect it from adversaries. Many SaaS-based Git providers allow you to use **GNU Privacy Guard** (**GPG**) to digitally sign your commits and tags. This is important to further determine who committed the code to the repository. When signing your commits, you will also receive a *Verified* tag further showing that it was committed by a verified person.

You should use **Secure Shell** (**SSH**) keys in addition to MFA when authenticating to your code repositories. These two authentication methods will also help determine the user who authenticated the repository. You can then use SSH keys to transfer code between their local machine and the repository.

Once code is no longer required, it should be discarded. You may need to hold onto the code for a number of years before it can be discarded. This will require that you store it in an encrypted volume offsite somewhere for safekeeping. You will also want to ensure that the code is no longer available to your developers. This will help ensure that once the code has been decommissioned, it can no longer be used.

The next control family is all about availability in the environment.

Technology Infrastructure Resilience (PR.IP)

We will take a look at ways of segmenting your network to promote better isolation of resources while also determining ways of ensuring high availability. This will include physical components such as the power source and temperature of the environment.

PR.IP-01

Networks and environments are protected from unauthorized logical access and usage.

Flat networks are easy to set up, easy to maintain, and easy to compromise. Why? Because you are not filtering any traffic between two or more endpoints. Once an IT resource is compromised, the adversary can then use that equipment to pivot to other systems within the network.

Several regulatory compliance bodies, including PCI, have mandated that organizations segment their PCI cardholder data environments from the rest of the network. Without proper segmentation, the entire server-based network, not just the systems that hold onto PCI data, is susceptible to PCI requirements.

Best practices involve segmenting your entire network. If you have a server network, a user network, and a wireless network, these should all be separated by a firewall, restricting access to the other network. Organizations should also have a guest network, one that will be completely isolated from the rest of the environment.

Internet of Things, operational technology, and even mobile devices should have their own networks, too. The point is that the interface for the VLAN should reside on a firewall or router, which will allow for stateful packet inspection of the traffic going from one resource to the next.

Once you have created various networks within your LAN, ensure proper firewall rules or **access control lists** (**ACLs**) are created, restricting access to other networks. This includes egress rules too. Does your Active Directory controller need internet access? Probably not. If this is the case, then the firewall rule should block all outbound traffic.

PR.IP-02

The organization's technology assets are protected from environmental threats.

You will want to do extensive research prior to opening and operating your own data center or choosing one to put your resources in. Data centers are spread across the globe; however, you must ensure adequate protections are in place.

For example, organizations may place their IT resources in areas of the country or globe that are susceptible to hurricanes, droughts, floods, and even wildfires. These threats all play into the operations of the data center itself. If you place your resources in a data center, in a location that has hurricanes, you have to worry about the power grid going down or possible flooding. The desert may sound like a great place to open a data center; however, you have to worry about excessive heat, lack of cooling, and possible rolling blackouts to conserve energy. There are different classes of data centers as well, which you should pay attention to.

Look for redundancy when selecting your data center. It should have multiple **internet service providers** (**ISPs**), generators, and redundant **heating, ventilation, and air conditioning** (**HVAC**). Some data centers may be across state lines and can hook up to two or more electric grids. All of these should be considered when selecting the right location for your resources and information.

PR.IP-03

Mechanisms are implemented to achieve resilience requirements in normal and adverse situations.

When evaluating a system for security, you also need to take into account the **confidentiality, integrity, and availability (CIA)** triad. Part of the **CIA triad** is availability and how that impacts a given IT resource. During your security review, ask business-related questions about requirements and availability. This is to ensure that the system is up and running as expected.

Some devices do not need to be up and running 24x7, and that is perfectly fine. However, there are many business-related systems that do require this, such as web servers that act as storefronts or databases that need to be running all the time. Ensure that you have redundancies built into the environment in order to meet business needs.

A system may need to be load-balanced or have the ability to switch over to a different resource if the primary goes offline. Network appliances and servers will have the capability to house multiple power supplies and will allow you to connect those power supplies to different **power distribution units (PDU)**. You may also have redundant network interface cards and have those load-balance across multiple switches in a switch stack. Or you could just have a single server running off of a single PDU in a basement somewhere. It is all a matter of balancing the risk and what course of action you choose if that system goes offline.

PR.IP-04

Adequate resource capacity to ensure availability is maintained.

You will want to set up resource monitoring to meet this control objective. This can be through the use of SNMP or other monitoring-related protocols. You will want to ensure that you are meeting business expectations for both current and future requirements. For example, consider an online retailer that has two systems in a redundant cluster that can keep up most of the year except for when there is a surge. This can happen around holiday time, and the retailer may have to look at expanding the number of resources allocated.

You can also monitor network capacity to ensure that you have enough bandwidth to meet demands. Large organizations usually have at least one if not more data centers that have backup requirements. If you are replicating those backups across the WAN, ensure that you have enough bandwidth capacity for the replication to happen appropriately. Setting up SNMP to monitor network interface traffic will help in these situations. You may also need to throw more CPU or memory into a system due to a lack of resources or new requirements.

Build metrics or plans around future capacity as well. If you have SNMP set up for monitoring, look at historical graphs to determine whether additional resources are required. Also, look at past capacity plans to determine whether you are on the right track or you need to add more resources – for example, utilizing a load balancer to spread the load of computational transactions across several servers. This will ensure that systems do not become overloaded and fail due to inadequate capacity.

Summary

This chapter covered quite a bit, so why not recap? We initially covered identity: what it is, how to assign unique identities, and how to protect them. Each user should have a unique identifier and password to protect online service accounts. We also took this a step further and introduced MFA, which further protects the identity from being compromised while providing enhanced validation or proof that the identity belongs to a specific user. Securing data on disk, in transit, and in use was also discussed. These technologies utilize some form of encryption, whether that is utilizing full-disk encryption or TLS for in-flight data transactions. We also discussed the need to protect information resident in memory so that adversaries do not gain access to it while the file is opened or in use.

Backups were also discussed and their need to be secured and encrypted. Backups contain all of your information, from every IT resource, so extra care should be taken when considering transfer and storage. Look at what you can do to secure backups by ensuring that they are encrypted and stored in a secured location. The backups themselves should also be checked periodically to ensure that you can restore them successfully.

Next, we looked at the maintenance of hardware and software. This calls for a CAB. This board is responsible for the management and oversight of all changes that occur in the environment. Each change on an IT resource should be tracked to ensure that configuration drift does not occur, or when it does, that too can be tracked and incorporated into the system. When monitoring for configuration drift, you want to ensure that it does not occur without the prior knowledge of someone in IT.

We also want to ensure that the devices we are protecting are available when needed. Mechanisms such as load balancers and monitoring protocols such as SNMP can be utilized to ensure that systems are performing properly and we can monitor them for resource issues.

In the next chapter, we will take a look at the Detect function. This function is meant to help us determine the various types of detections that we may encounter, what to do with them, and the importance of sending them to an SIEM system or log collector.

References

1. `https://www.knowbe4.com/press/security-awareness-training-reduces-phishing-susceptibility-by-75`

6

Detect

In *Chapter 5*, we learned about the *Protect* function. In that chapter, we discovered ways to prove an identity. This includes not only proofing these identities in person but also ensuring that the method of authentication is commensurate with the level of risk the organization is willing to take. While a username and password combination used to be good enough for authentication purposes, it no longer is.

We also discussed ways of protecting your data. This includes data that is stored on disks, transferred in flight, or used by the system. To adequately protect your data, we must look at the use of encryption to safeguard against attacks such as **man-in-the-middle** or memory scraping.

Lastly, we touched on building resiliency requirements for your systems. There should be service-level agreements between IT and the business to ensure that business requirements are being met. If a system goes down, and it is critical to the business, how long will it take to get it back up and running again? Should you build redundancy into the service or application being used?

The Detect function is centered around the visibility of threats, vulnerabilities, indicators of compromise, and anomalies. We will discuss how to detect them, the methods that could be used to perform this detection, and what you should have in your network to monitor for these types of threats.

In this chapter, we will cover the following topics:

- Continuous monitoring
- Adverse event analysis

Let us get to it!

Continuous monitoring (DE.CM)

It should be possible to monitor all IT resources within the environment. Not only does this include the need to monitor the resources and configuration drift but also the need to monitor the security and integrity of the resources. This can include monitoring for system anomalies, file integrity checking, and monitoring of log files.

This monitoring should be all-encompassing, meaning we are monitoring more than just the network. We are monitoring systems, servers, appliances, and the software running on the device. We can look at user behavior, data loss prevention, and third-party vendors.

DE.CM-01

Networks and network services are monitored to find potentially adverse events.

Chances are, you have wireless set up in your environment, but is it protected? Are you using some type of authentication when your users try to authenticate to the network? Are you detecting rogue access points to protect your network from unauthorized access? This goes further than just wireless networks though; we must also monitor our local and wide area networks.

Organizations rely heavily on the internet to conduct business and use shared services. You may have a centralized or distributed datacenter where services are consumed from remote locations. For example, your main and satellite offices may have more than one **Internet Service Provider** (**ISP**). To utilize multiple ISPs effectively and efficiently, you would also need multiple firewalls and network switching equipment. All of these use specialized protocols to maintain high availability. Also, the communication channels should be protected by isolated VLANs and encryption.

You should be protecting your network from rogue wireless access points that can be connected to your network. These rogue access points could contain weak passwords or encryption, or they may be wide open without any protections. This leaves a hole in your network. Monitor for rogue access points and when one is detected, shut it down.

Protocols such as `802.1x` allow for authentication to occur prior to gaining access to the network. Without passing the right credentials, a network device is denied access to the network. This protocol can also be used for wireless authentication. By utilizing `802.1x` authentication, you can utilize the usernames and passwords used in Active Directory or similar types of identity stores.

Monitor the network for attacks against these and other protocols as this could be an indicator of a compromised IT resource. Implement IDS/IPS sensors throughout the network to ensure that you are able to pick up on malicious traffic. Network sniffers and netflows are just a couple of the ways that you can pick up on this traffic with little to no cost.

DE.CM-02

The physical environment is monitored to find potentially adverse events.

We previously discussed what you should do prior to allowing access to your datacenter. This included background checks, signatures for checking in at the front desk, and work orders stating a purpose for being there. This should all be reviewed on a regular basis.

You may have systems that are card readers for allowing employees to gain access to certain floors or doors within a building. These card readers store information about who the person is, as well as timestamps for when they entered and exited the building. Logs from these systems can be sent to your **Security Information and Event Management (SIEM)** system for analysis and combined with end user analytics to develop patterns for your users. This can help understand any abnormalities better.

Monitoring can also help with alerting on natural events. For instance, if you get a lot of rain and are susceptible to flooding, you can place sensors around the building to detect water. Sensors can also be put in place to monitor the temperature of the server room as servers typically do not like the heat.

DE.CM-03

Personnel activity and technology usage are monitored to find potentially adverse events.

End user behavioral analytics tools do serve a purpose in highly secured environments. You may want to monitor activity on social media sites to monitor what is being posted on the internet. This is also a great tool to detect whether employees are going to job posting boards. This can pose a possibility that your intellectual property or other sensitive information could be walking out the door with that employee.

Monitor your network and VPN logs to see where your employees are located. I have heard stories of organizations being affected by adversaries logging in to their VPNs from other countries. It was when the organization began to run queries against the logs that they detected successful logins from known bad actors. This raised alarms within IT and cybersecurity to react to the situation.

DE.CM-06

External service provider activities and services are monitored to find potentially adverse events.

While there are several paid-for services that will provide this type of information, there are also things that you can do internally. We want to monitor our external third parties for breaches and vulnerabilities, reduce our attack surface, and review the logs from our third-party services.

If you have vendors accessing your environment, you must review and approve foreign devices connected to the network. These foreign devices are not under your IT or cybersecurity control. As these devices are in your environment, you have to ensure that they are as secure as possible.

Several third-party evaluation services will monitor your external vendors and report metrics based on their security posture. These services provide a grade or score based on signals and configurations of their external footprint. These reports are meant to highlight their security posture as well as provide alerts if one of your vendors is breached or has a number of critical vulnerabilities.

Utilize the results from these scanning services to increase your security posture by working with your third-party vendors. Your organization may not be the only one with the capability to work with your data. The business may have also partnered with third parties to store, process, or transfer your information as well. This is a shared responsibility when reviewing access to your data and all should have a vested interest in protecting your information.

DE.CM-09

Computing hardware and software, runtime environments, and their data are monitored to find potentially adverse events.

This control requires that we monitor our entire environment. We will want to pull logs from our email provider, which is often our office suite as well. We will also want to see our web, operating systems, and even our hardware logs. This will also require us to review our attack surface and minimize it as much as possible.

Perform scans across your network to determine what is connected to it. You can use tools such as NMAP to perform this. Take this information and run it against your CMDB to determine what is known and unknown to the network. NMAP will also perform initial software scans to help determine what type of services are running on the device.

Monitor your hardware for signs of tampering. This will provide valuable information when determining whether someone has compromised the physical hardware of the device. Look for signs of wear and tear, whether a seal was broken, or other signs of tampering. Some anti-tampering systems will also sound an alarm if physical hardware has been damaged.

You will also want to monitor your environment for signs of high throughput on the network. This can often lead to either resolving a misconfiguration or identifying signs of data exfiltration. If you have jobs that run at certain times of the day or days of the week, look for anomalies of off-peak times of usage. If you see spikes in usage during off-peak times, this could mean that someone or something is not working as intended or could be something far worse.

Adverse event analysis (DE.AE)

Now that we are pulling in information as far as signals from third-party vendors and collecting log files, we need to analyze them. This will require a person or a team to not only monitor the log files coming in but also tune tools to understand the log files being ingested.

If you have large, distributed data centers, this may also require that the deployment of log collectors is architected such that you never lose log files. This is necessary to protect your environment in the event of a network failure. If your network loses connectivity to the location where the log collector resides, you may also lose those logs. Let us take a look at this control family.

DE.AE-02

Potential adverse events are analyzed to better understand associated activities.

You must ensure that your devices are sending logs to a centralized log collector or a SIEM. A SIEM is used to collect logs and perform analysis on them. However, you may need to have a dedicated person or a team of people to manage it. Most SIEMs do not come pre-built with rules; you may need to develop your own. Several organizations have outsourced their logging requirements to a **Managed**

Security Provider (**MSP**) to manage their SIEM for them. This is because organizations do not always have the resources to train and maintain the analysts that run them.

A SIEM, much like a computer, is only as good as the programs that run on it. In this case, it is the signatures that need to be developed in order to pick up on certain patterns. This could be multiple failed authentication attempts to an account that was taken over by an adversary. It is important to train your staff on how to care for and feed a SIEM if you decide to deploy one internally rather than going with an external SIEM. Without the necessary skills to run it, it may not provide you with the information you need.

Periodically perform manual reviews of your logging tools, too. This is to make sure that the systems running the queries against the logs are still providing the information needed. Continually run through the PDCA to pick up on issues and make improvements to the SIEM. If you are not tuning and creating new rules to pick up on threats, you may be missing out on crucial information about your environment.

DE.AE-03

Information is correlated from multiple sources.

A SIEM is only as good as the information being sent to it. What does this mean? This means that you should be sending logs from all IT resources and cloud-based applications. This may require that you have multiple log collectors set up and distributed across your network and cloud service provider.

You may also want to transfer your logs to multiple destinations for backup purposes. SIEMs typically only store 30 to 90 days' worth of logs. There are compliance requirements that could stipulate that you keep a year's worth of logs. You cannot just discard them once you have run out of space on the SIEM. Review the business requirements prior to engaging in purchasing a SIEM or a managed service and ensure that you are meeting the business requirements.

DE.AE-04

The estimated impact and scope of adverse events are determined.

Create policies and procedures for how to determine the impact of an adverse event. We must understand the impact of the detected event from our logging and alerting tools as this will direct how we respond to an incident. Before we can understand how the event will impact us, we must have a discussion about business risk and how to respond to it.

A discussion about business risk is a must when deciding how to respond. Without this understanding, you will not know how to effectively respond to a given event. For example, if you require multifactor authentication but have to deactivate it for a given task to work, how would you respond to an event? Could you block the event from happening again? Would you be able to respond to the event at all? These are business decisions that should be made.

Once business risk is understood, we can place it into policies and procedures. These documents then get distributed throughout the organization so there is a common understanding of how to deal with the events being received.

DE.AE-06

Information on adverse events is provided to authorized staff and tools.

Now that we have discussed business risk, as well as written policies and procedures, we can tune our tools and automate our responses. Security operations staff should be in the know when alerts are generated and sent for evaluation. When an alert is generated, you can also have it open work orders automatically for tracking purposes.

Depending on the size of the organization, you may have one or more analysts who work in an operations setting. With the plethora of alerts that can come in from a SIEM, it is important that the SIEM is tuned appropriately so that it is not just a bunch of noise the analysts have to sift through. You will need actionable alerts that staff will have to go through and make some type of decision about what to do next.

Many ITSM tools will allow you to open a work order automatically; use this to your advantage. If your SIEM detects an anomaly, use the SIEM to send an alert or notification through an API to open work orders on your behalf. You can also have notifications set up to notify you through SMS when there are adverse events.

Your SOC staff should also have close ties with your incident response team. This is to ensure that events are escalated as necessary. Again, rely on your incident response policies and procedures for this. There should be certain thresholds established when alerting on events.

DE.AE-07

Cyber threat intelligence and other contextual information are integrated into the analysis.

We have touched on this quite a bit. However, the information that is received from an ISAC, CISA, or other third-party threat intelligence is what is needed for this control. See how you can dump this information into a SIEM or other analysis tools so that you can get a clear picture of your overall risk posture.

Obtain tools that will provide you with a clear picture of your risk posture. These tools could be configured to bring all of your identified risks into one centralized location. For example, look for tools that can bring in the information collected in your CMDB, with vulnerability information, along with attack information collected from the CISA KEV or EPSS. This will help with identifying your risk and how to tackle your remediation efforts.

DE.AE-08

Incidents are declared when adverse events meet the defined incident criteria.

We will need to rely on our policies and procedures to meet this requirement. Ensure the documentation has defined responses depending on the threshold of the event received. You will not be able to define a response for every single event. However, you can generalize your response to a handful of events. You can then develop responses for the events that occur most frequently.

Once an incident has been identified, your security analysts will need to work with your incident response team to contain and eradicate the event from your network. This will most likely be a combination of the IR team and the analysts working toward a common solution.

You may also want to record the information from every incident regardless of whether it was a true incident or a false positive. This will help improve your policies and procedures and your incident response plans. After each event, run a **lessons learned** or an **after-action** review for continual improvement.

Summary

There was a lot to cover in this relatively short chapter. We learned that we need to have proper auditing and logging in place to capture events from all of our IT resources. We also learned that we need to capture logs from our third-party vendors, SaaS applications, web application firewalls, and network equipment, and pump those into a SIEM for log correlation and analysis.

We learned that we should also monitor physical hardware to ensure that it is not tampered with. This can include alarms that go off, anti-tampering seals that may have been broken, to monitoring it through CCTVs. We should also capture badge readers to determine when someone entered and left the building

Furthermore, we learned that SIEMs are tools to which we will send all our logs for analysis. This analysis is needed to understand our risks based on the events received. A SIEM is only as good as the logic built into it, so we also need rules to detect adverse events. Organizations will typically outsource the operations of the SIEM and other functionality to a trusted third party that has the expertise.

We also need to have discussions around business risk so we can respond to events appropriately, as we learned in this chapter. The decisions made around risk should then be placed into a policy document and signed off on by management. Once approved, it can then be sent to the rest of the organization for their review.

In the next chapter, we will discuss how we respond to an adverse event. It will include how we evaluate, label, and remediate the event once it is detected in the environment.

7
Respond

In *Chapter 6*, we learned about the *Detect* function. The Detect function is all about how we detect adverse events within our environment. We first began to discuss detection across the network. These included detections of our networking protocols such as BGP for routing or VRRP for our device failovers. We also discussed why encrypting these protocols is important along with the possibility of isolating the communications across out-of-band networks.

In the last chapter, we also talked about the need for logging and developing rules to detect adverse events. This included the need to push all of your logs to a SIEM tool for analysis. However, analysis is only as good as the rules used to detect these events.

Once we have configured all our IT resources to send their logs to a logging tool, and analyzed the results, we must do something about it. Thresholds need to be created in order to determine the severity of the event that was detected. We also need to develop policies and procedures for how we intend to respond to that incident. There should be **Service Level Agreements** (**SLAs**) to ensure that our response times fall within business needs.

In this chapter, we will discuss the Respond function and its importance for **Incident Response** (**IR**). Once a detection has been made, and its severity has been determined, we must respond to it in some way. That is where the importance of this function comes in. Not all events will become an incident. However, how would you know without first establishing the criteria to make this determination?

We will need to continue to develop our policies and procedures as well. As we begin to bring in feeds from our log files and write rules for analysis, we constantly need to evaluate the threat. This will all have to be documented for the IR team to know and understand how to respond to the threat.

In this chapter, we will cover the following topics:

- Incident management (RS.MA)
- Incident analysis (RS.AN)
- Incident Reponse reporting and communication (RS.CO)
- Incident mitigation (RS.MI)

Let us jump into incident management.

Incident management (RS.MA)

In this control family, we will need to create an IR plan. This plan will encompass several aspects of how to respond to an incident. We will need to write policies and procedures for how to discover an incident, determine the threat level, and respond accordingly.

RS.MA-01

The incident response plan is executed in coordination with relevant third parties once an incident is declared.

Throughout the last few chapters, we have discussed the need to work with vendors and trusted third parties when an incident occurs. If you have outsourced security services to a **Managed Service Provider** (**MSP**), then you should work with them to develop an IR playbook. This playbook will be executed when an incident is declared.

The playbook is a step-by-step procedure for how to handle a given situation. For example, if you experience an account takeover scenario, then there are steps that you should take to minimize the risks associated. Many playbooks are created using Microsoft Visio or equivalent for the development of the process. It is a visual representation of the procedure written down on paper.

You will also need to hold tabletop exercises with your vendors and trusted third parties. This will build the muscle memory needed to react to certain situations when they do arise. When minutes count during an incident, you do not want to waste time. This muscle memory will help reduce the amount of time needed to respond to an incident.

Create a roles and responsibilities matrix to assist in determining who is responsible for what. First, you will need a lead: someone in authority to take charge of an incident when one does occur. The lead will orchestrate the response to contain the attack. You should have members of various teams involved, such as networking specialists, server administrators, help desk workers, and even those outside of IT.

Rely on your policies and procedures that have been developed to help determine the thresholds of an incident and its impact on the business. These documents should spell out what needs to be done to prevent an incident from spreading. Next, you will want to work on eradicating malicious activity from your environment. The policies and procedures should also detail what is and is not considered an incident. Not all events become incidents. However, all incidents started as events.

RS.MA-02

Incident reports are triaged and validated.

FIPS 199 details the criteria for categorizing events and applies severity levels to them. These are ranked as low, moderate, and high, and are stated as follows:

- **Low**: There is a limited adverse effect on the organization due to a loss of confidentiality, integrity, or availability

- **Moderate**: There is a serious adverse effect on the organization due to a loss of confidentiality, integrity, or availability

- **High**: There is a serious or catastrophic adverse effect on the organization due to a loss of confidentiality, integrity, or availability

These criteria will come in handy when determining how to respond to an incident. If an incident is low, you will know how quickly you should respond (if at all), whereas you will know that a high incident requires you to respond immediately.

You will also want to have reports generated and reviewed to determine which events became incidents. These reports should also spell out what should not have been reported as an incident. This will save you and your team valuable time not only when you respond to an incident but also when a reported incident turns out not to be one, so you can fail fast.

Once an incident has been validated, work to contain the incident as soon as possible. When containment has been completed, at least to the best of your ability, begin work to eradicate the adverse event.

A great example of incident report writing can be found here [1].

RS.MA-03

Incidents are categorized and prioritized.

While we categorized our adverse events in RS.MA-02, low, moderate, and high categories are not enough. Each adverse event should be placed into its own bucket or types of attacks. For example, we could categorize them as one of the following:

- Business email compromise

- Account takeover

- Ransomware

- Breach

As we have developed SLAs, created impact thresholds, and learned about the scope of the incident, we can then prioritize how we respond to it. You may target your Active Directory servers as they are of the highest importance within your IT resources. From there, you may decide to prioritize your databases or SCCM environments depending on the type of attack it is. This information should be contained within your CMDB or a similar tool.

When responding to an incident, it may also be necessary to take a step back and observe what they are doing. By doing this, you can gather a lot of intelligence on how an adversary conducts an attack. This information can then be turned into playbooks for future attack remediation. Do not do this for long, however, as eventually the attackers will get what they want.

RS.MA-04

Incidents are escalated or elevated as needed.

With this control, you must monitor the status of the incident or incidents that you may be experiencing at any given time. If an incident is out of control and you need assistance, you need to escalate the issues being faced to others either inside or outside the organization.

If you are escalating internally, you may need to call in additional employees to assist with troubleshooting a given issue or help with containing an outbreak. This could include those on the networking or server side of IT whose expertise will be needed. If you are escalating externally, you will need help from trusted third parties such as a managed security provider, ISAC, or law enforcement. For example, you may have your firewalls managed by the MSP and will need to get a hold of them quickly to block a threat coming into your network. Having contacts at these facilities is beneficial when needing assistance.

Leverage your after-action reviews to better understand whether the process is working as intended. An after-action review is meant to highlight deficiencies in your response plan. Take into account how the response occurred and whether it was appropriate for the situation.

RS.MA-05

The criteria for initiating incident recovery are applied.

Once the incident has been contained, and the threat has been eradicated, look for possible key areas where you can begin recovery. This is where you will need to have runbooks created for various types of incidents within your organization. These runbooks should be diversified into multiple categories, much like we did in RS.MA-03.

A runbook for business email compromise or account takeover will look different than the runbooks for ransomware. Each runbook should also discuss the containment and eradication phases of the incident. Having this information will assist with cleaning up the incident while trying to minimize the amount of downtime caused by the event.

Not all incidents are the same and they should not be treated as such. A business email compromise may or may not disrupt service for an employee or the entire company. However, a ransomware attack has the possibility to take down a network for extended periods of time. This type of attack will cause disruptions of service and it is up to you and your team to minimize the amount of disruption. (For more information on how to create IR playbooks, take a look at [2] in the *References* section.)

Incident analysis (RS.AN)

In this control family, we will discuss the actions or steps you need to take during and after an incident has occurred. This will include recording all the steps taken during the incident, performing an after-action review, and preserving a chain of custody for the incident report being generated.

RS.AN-03

Analysis is performed to determine what has taken place during an incident and the root cause of the incident.

In this control, we are trying to determine the steps that led up to the incident. This will require that we create a timeline of the incident itself, from when the event was determined to be an incident, to the steps that the IR team took to contain and eradicate the incident from the environment. Creating this timeline will also help us determine the root cause of the incident.

In the development of the timeline, take the decisions that lead to making the event an incident into account. There was a decision that was made to enact the IR team and begin developing the response to the incident. Record everything in the timeline as well. From decisions that were made to contain the incident to conversations that were had, everything should be recorded.

Also, record the decisions that were made in regard to the various systems and services that are in the environment. For example, if an adversary took advantage of a vulnerability, was that vulnerability discovered within the environment? Was there an exploit from the CISA KEV that pertained to your environment? If so, what was the decision that was made to either mitigate or accept the vulnerability?

This timeline is outside of the policies and procedures that were developed. However, the discussion around the creation of a timeline should be part of those documents. It is critical that you maintain this timeline of events to help paint the picture of what your IR team did and the decisions that were made.

RS.AN-06

Actions performed during an investigation are recorded, and the records integrity and provenance are preserved.

We also want to preserve the integrity of the timeline to ensure that it was not altered in any way. This will come in need when we begin to discuss the chain of custody of the document and prevent alterations of the document once it is completed. You will want to ensure that the timeline is as accurate as possible in case it is to be submitted to law enforcement.

To ensure the integrity of the document, we can also use a hashing algorithm on the document itself. As we discussed previously, a hash is a digital fingerprint of the document, and that fingerprint changes when the document is altered in any way. This will protect the integrity of the document. However, it will not cover the authenticity of the document. To do this, you will need to leverage a digital signature. A digital signature will prove both the authenticity and integrity of the document as the person signing the timeline will need to be in possession of the private encryption key.

The private key used to generate the digital signature must be protected at all costs. If you lose possession of the private key, anyone could impersonate you and digitally sign the document without your knowledge. The digital signature will then be verified by your public key. The public key can be shared with anyone and will need to be shared in order to verify the signature is valid.

RS.AN-07

Incident data and metadata are collected, and their integrity and provenance are preserved.

The definition of metadata is data about data. Metadata includes everything that made up the event, which includes timestamps, IP addresses, sources, destinations, and the identity of the person who made the event. This information should also be captured and placed into the timeline to better understand the characteristics that made up the event. This information will come in handy for chain-of-custody requirements.

Ensure that all the logs that are generated go to a centralized logging solution such as a log correlation engine or SIEM. You want to have all of your logs going to a centralized system in order to gain a full picture of the events that occurred. Having this metadata as part of the overall logs will provide additional insight into the adverse event and how it occurred. Eventually, we will want to understand the root cause of the incident; this will help with understanding what happened.

RS.AN-08

An incident's magnitude is estimated and validated.

The determination of an incident's magnitude should be part of your policies and procedures documentation. We can calculate the incident's impact on the organization by leveraging FIPS 199 and how that applies to the confidentiality, integrity, and availability of IT resources. This classification is helpful when determining the magnitude of an incident and what you and your team should do in response. For example, you could have a database that is down that only affects a certain amount of users within the company. On the other hand, you could have a system-wide outage affecting all users within the organization. Which one would take precedence?

When filing the IR report, ensure that this has been documented for historical purposes. A report should include not only the description, the players involved, and a timeline, but also the magnitude of the impact the incident had. In the previous database example, you could have a low impact if the database outage only affected 5% of the workforce, whereas a high impact would be warranted in the event a database was down for the entire company. Additional information can be found here: [3].

We will also need to finalize the source or the root cause of the incident and how that impacted the company. Take this information and create new or alter current runbooks to reduce the time it takes to respond to future incidents. This is important as it will help reduce the amount of time it takes to respond to future incidents.

Incident response reporting and communication (RS.CO)

This control family is all about getting the word out when an incident strikes. It is not just internal stakeholders that you will have to notify though. You will also need to notify external stakeholders and maybe even regulatory bodies. States and the federal government have breach notification laws whereby you are required to notify those affected by a certain date or within a certain time limit. This date could be one day to one month after determining whether it was a breach or not.

RS.CO-02

Internal and external stakeholders are notified of incidents.

Your policies and procedures should state if and when you notify others of a data breach or other adverse event that has affected your company. There should be thresholds that dictate whom to speak with and when after an event has occurred. There also needs to be a determination of whether the event affected others and is considered a breach of confidential information.

For example, PCI 12.10 requires that you have a thorough IR plan in place and that it has been tested. The requirements also state that you must have a data backup process and a business continuity plan in place. Depending on your merchant, they also may have additional steps or requirements such as how much time you have to notify them of a breach.

Another example is that the **Securities and Exchange Commission (SEC)** introduced new rules that require publicly traded companies to send out notifications within four days of a material breach. This means that if your company has determined that a breach of sensitive information is considered material, you have four days from the time you deemed it material to send out a notification.

You may need to work with the executive leadership team, legal department, and outside counsel to assist in the determination of a data breach. Also, utilize law enforcement and the **Internet Crime Complaint Center** (**IC3.gov**) to notify the FBI when a breach or other adverse event has struck your organization.

RS.CO-03

Information is shared with designated internal and external stakeholders.

For this control, you will need to rely on your policies and procedures along with any contracts or legal documents you may have with third parties. Each of these documents should have SLAs for how and when to communicate this information to all your stakeholders. You will also need to develop a crisis communication plan for how to speak with these various groups.

Review any contracts that you have with third-party vendors. The contracts will more than likely have verbiage around how to communicate with the vendor and when. As mentioned previously, several regulatory requirements state that you must notify them within a certain timeframe to be considered *in compliance*. You may face hefty fines if notification is beyond that timeframe. Vendors and customers may have similar language in their contracts. Be sure to have your legal department review them to ensure that you and your organization are maintaining their agreed-upon SLAs.

Your communications (or similar) department should also create a **Crisis Communication Plan** (**CCP**). This communication plan is to be used if and when a serious incident has occurred. Thresholds should be established in the policies and procedures documents for when to activate or use the plan. You may have several CCPs depending on the audience you are communicating with. Work with your communications department to ensure that these documents are created.

Incident mitigation (RS.MI)

In this control family, we discuss how to mitigate or contain and eradicate the adverse event from the environment. We will need to work with third parties or trusted vendors in our environment possibly to perform techniques to understand our attack surface and how the event happened to begin with.

RS.MI-01

Incidents are contained.

We need to contain the event and prevent it from spreading across the network. This can include the use of firewalls, closing off ports between network segments, and applying patches. If we know which vulnerability was taken advantage of, we can look at our vulnerability management system to report whether other systems are affected. Once this is determined, we can move forward with patching or putting in compensating controls. We can also determine whether we can live without the service being offered and turn off the system.

We also need to engage with third-party vendors for their assistance. By reaching out to your MSP, law enforcement, and ISACs, you can get their assistance to see whether those services have had other customers affected by a similar issue. You can also work with a forensics firm to help understand the root cause of the problem. All of this information can be critical to containing the incident.

RS.MI-02

Incident are eradicated.

Now that the event has been contained, we need to remove it from the environment. Again, look at your vulnerability management system to determine whether there are similar vulnerabilities affecting other systems. This can be a good indication of where the attack may go next. You should also create your interim corrective action and permanent corrective action plans.

The **Interim Corrective Action** (**ICA**) plan can start to be developed during the containment phase of your response, but it can also be developed when you begin to eradicate it. In the short term, the ICA is meant to capture what was performed when containing and eradicating an adverse event. This can be temporary fixes such as enacting additional firewall rules or turning off a service. An ICA could also include patching vulnerabilities to further prevent an infection from occurring or spreading.

A **Permanent Corrective Action (PCA)** is a little more involved and typically gets implemented after the event has occurred. A PCA could require that you obtain funding for new tools or implement a new process. These can be long-term projects that cannot be implemented within a short period of time. A PCA is meant to be a permanent solution to resolve a gap or finding.

Continue to include your MSP, law enforcement, ISACs, and any other third-party resource you may use. They will help guide you through the process of what you need to do to get you back up and running again. The more brain power, the better. This will make you better while helping inform others within the community of what is going on.

After the incident or event has subsided, begin to look at what was implemented during the ICA and remove any temporary mitigation measures. This is meant to get you back to a known good environment and fall within the previously established baselines. This is, however, also the time to adjust your baselines if a new monitoring service was implemented as part of your PCA.

Summary

In this chapter, we discussed several topics related to how to respond to an adverse event. We covered quite a bit in regard to what information to capture, how to capture it, and when it should be captured. Not only do we need to capture all of the information regarding the incident but we must also protect it by using different types of encryption.

We learned that it is important to capture all the information necessary to walk through the steps again if we ever need to. This includes the people involved in the incident, the locations, and what occurred during that time. We also learned that we need to capture the metadata about the event as well. This includes the timestamps, IP addresses, usernames, and duration. We also need to require that the event in the log has a sequence number associated with it. This way, we know that logs are not missing.

We must protect the incident logs as well, as we learned in this chapter. This requires the use of encryption. We can use hashing algorithms to ensure the integrity of the document, or digital signatures to verify authenticity. In many cases, SIEMs will create a hash of every event that comes in, further proving the integrity of the logged event.

We discussed the importance of creating various crisis communication plans for discussing issues with both internal and external stakeholders. We may also have the responsibility of reporting an incident to our vendors, customers, and regulatory bodies. For example, HIPAA states that you have to notify those affected within 60 days. You will need a plan for how to communicate and respond to those issues.

Lastly, we discussed ICAs and PCAs. An ICA is an interim or temporary mitigation that was put in place to contain and eradicate an event. An ICA could be temporary firewall rules or the shutdown of systems and services. These would only be temporary and may need to be taken out after the event has subsided.

A PCA is a permanent solution that is put in place. A PCA could be project-based, taking months to implement. These can also be newly created policies and procedures. It may take time to fully plan out all the PCAs required to mitigate the event and prevent it from happening again, as we learned in this chapter.

In the next chapter, we discuss the *Recover* function. This function is meant to provide guidance for how we recover from an incident. This can include restoration of backups and ensuring that our systems are back to normal operations.

References

1. `https://www.hackthebox.com/blog/writing-incident-response-report-template`

2. `https://www.atlassian.com/incident-management/incident-response/how-to-create-an-incident-response-playbook`

3. `https://www.atlassian.com/incident-management/kpis/severity-levels`

8
Recover

We covered how to respond to an incident in *Chapter 7*. This included collecting log files, creating policies and procedures for how to categorize and respond to an incident, creating a crisis communications plan, and developing an ICA and PCA. To wrap all of that up, we need to create documentation or a synopsis of the event and what occurred. This timeline will include several types of information and must be protected.

First, we need to analyze the log files that come into our SIEM to determine whether or not the incident is to be considered an adverse event. We must develop rules in our SIEM to pick up on signatures or characteristics of adverse events within our environment. Once a signature has been triggered, we need to determine the threshold or criticality of the event.

If the event has been determined as an incident, we need to enact our incident response plan. This plan will engage the incident response team to begin triaging the incident. This will require the development of an ICA and PCA. The ICA is used an interim solution and can include temporary solutions to contain and eradicate the incident.

The ICA can be used as a temporary solution to contain the incident. This can include temporary firewall rules or the deactivation of services. The PCA provides permanent solutions to be implemented to prevent future incidents from occurring. A PCA could be a long-term project to implement a solution or change a process.

Now we will look at the last function of the NIST CSF, **Recover**. For this, we will dive into what is needed to recover from an incident. This will include the execution of your recovery process, the restoration of backups, and verifying that the environment is back to a known working state. We will also need to communicate our activities to internal and external stakeholders.

In this chapter, we will cover the following topics:

- Incident recovery plan execution
- Incident recovery communication

Let us check out this final function!

Incident recovery plan execution (RC.RP)

In this control family, we will discuss what to do when recovering from an incident. This includes enacting your recovery plan to bring systems back up to a known running state. This will require that you follow your recovery plan, restore your backups, and establish existing or new baselines for your IT resources.

RC.RP-01

> *The recovery portion of the incident response plan is executed once initiated from the incident response process.*

Now that we have implemented our ICA and PCAs, it is time to start the actual recovery process of our incident response plan. This will entail utilizing our recovery plans to get systems back up and running again with newly established baselines. We may need to also include internal and external stakeholders to do this.

As part of your incident response plans, there should be a way to instruct your IT team to begin work on recreating your environment. There should be step-by-step instructions on how to recreate a system or IT resource and get it back to a known running state. This should include procedures on how to rebuild server or network equipment, where to grab the necessary software, and how to install it.

The network and application flow diagrams we previously made will come in handy to help us depict how the system works and its interdependencies. We will need to recreate our environment to those specifications. In addition to recreating our environment, we will need to also plan for our implementation of new systems and processes as part of our PCA.

Our PCA may require us to break apart old architecture and begin anew or augment our architecture due to new applications being used. Maybe we introduce a new control such as implementing vulnerability management or a new firewall. These new systems will need to be installed and configured and we'll need to ensure they are working as intended.

If a new process needs to be introduced, this would also be the time to do it. This may include additional firewall rules that need to be configured on the device or revisiting how we are patching our systems against vulnerabilities. A new process may include patching more frequently or setting up SLAs for when to patch certain vulnerabilities based on their criticality. All of this is important to understand when implementing new systems into the environment.

RC.RP-02

> *Recovery actions are selected, scoped, prioritized, and performed.*

As we begin our remediation, we must prioritize where we are placing our recovery efforts. We should review our ICA and PCAs and determine what should be implemented first and what can be placed on hold. This could be due to resource constraints or other issues that may be preventing us from implementing what is needed for recovery efforts.

Do a discovery of what is needed for recovery purposes and begin to build out a project plan for what to implement and when. This project plan should include what is important to get back up as quickly as possible and what can be done later on. The plan should include what can be done immediately and what will take time to get purchased and be put into production.

Work with your **executive leadership team** (ELT) to understand what is important for them to have implemented as well. The ELT and the business may want you to implement multifactor authentication before a new firewall is implemented, for example. These remediation efforts are all based on the amount of risk the business is willing to accept at that time.

There could also be multiple projects going on at the same time. You could have new firewalls going in while you work on process improvements. Plan out your projects so that they are implemented in accordance with how important they are to the business. This will also require that you have the right amount of resources in place as well.

Resources can come in a number of different types but they typically come down to financial or personnel constraints. Your recovery efforts will be dependent on both of these. You may not have the ability to implement a new control system due to budget constraints and it could get pushed back until more funding is available.

It may also come down to the amount of expertise you have on staff as this may require you to outsource the installation of new systems and services. It could also require that staff members are trained on the new systems being implemented. Both of these will require additional funding for the project. You could even have a trusted third party implement a new solution and train your staff at the same time.

RC.RP-03

*The integrity of backups and other restoration assets is verified before using them
for restoration.*

We have discussed the importance of ensuring that backups are performed on a regular basis. It is now time to test whether we are capable of restoring a backup to an IT resource. In addition to knowing whether we can restore a backup, we must also ensure that the files located in the backups are good and not corrupted. Through this process, we will have to rely on our encryption methods to determine whether we can successfully restore a system to normal.

There are several different methods of performing a backup. One of the more popular methods is the grandfather, father, and son approach. The intention of this approach is to perform backups on a regular basis while minimizing the amount of data we back up, reducing storage space.

The grandfather, father, and son approach to backups goes like this. We perform a full backup on a Sunday and incremental backups during the week. An incremental backup grabs only the changes to a given file; this is to reduce the overall amount of disk space being used. Once Sunday comes again, we perform another full backup and discard the incremental backups that were performed during the week. At the month's end, we do one more full backup and save that backup for the following month. The increments are called the sons, weekly backups are the fathers, and the monthly backups are the grandfather backups.

Each file that is backed up should be hashed to ensure that when there is a restore, we can verify that the file or image that is being restored matches the hash value. Not only should each file be hashed, but the entire backup itself should also have a hash value. Without a hash, we cannot validate that the backup being restored is an identical copy of what is in the backup.

Most of the time, an adversary will want to gain access to your backups and encrypt them with some type of ransomware with the intention of getting your company to pay the ransom payment in order to regain access to your backed-up files. There are several backup solutions out there that will back up your files into an immutable storage format.

Immutable storage is one where the file is written once and can never be overwritten. There are several benefits to this methodology. First and foremost, once a file is written, it cannot be modified in the storage of the backup. This means that ransomware cannot encrypt the files on the storage disk, maintaining the integrity of the backed-up file.

We should also stress the need to test your backups on a regular basis. By testing your backups, you can minimize the amount of time it takes to locate and restore the backups as it becomes second nature. You should also test whether you can restore an image to a filesystem and ensure that it was not corrupted during the process. These extra steps are to ensure that your backup process runs smoothly.

RC.RP-04

Critical mission functions and cybersecurity risk management are considered to establish post-incident operational norms.

We should have all of our systems in a CMDB, which tells us not only the system configuration items but also the criticality of the system. This information will come in handy when we begin our restoration efforts as we will want to know which systems to bring up first. To better understand the criticality of our systems, we will also want to have a conversation with the business to better understand what is considered critical to them.

As we restore our systems to a normal state, we again ensure the system meets the baselines that were established prior to the incident. In the event that this is a new system, or a reconfiguration of a system, we will need to work with the system owners to establish new baselines for the IT resource. This is all to ensure that the system is back to a known state.

Review system diagrams to get an idea of what interdependencies there are between two or more systems as well. You may have a database cluster with multiple servers connecting to it. You could have a failover on your network equipment or a special out-of-band network for management purposes. These should all be depicted in the diagrams.

You may also have monitoring systems in place to check on system performance and determine configuration drift. We must have these configured as well to assist us in determining whether the system is running as normal and the system is configured appropriately.

This will also require that you work with system owners to ensure that the system is back up and running as intended. This may require that the system goes through a series of checks before going into production. You do not want to implement a new or existing system without first checking whether or not it is working as intended.

RC.RP-05

The integrity of restored assets is verified, systems and services are restored, and normal operating status is confirmed.

This is where we perform our final tests before moving a system back into production. We need to verify that our ICA and PCAs have been implemented or are in the process of being implemented and that the event has been fully eradicated from our environment.

If we do not validate that the event or incident has been contained and eradicated from the environment, we face the chance of being re-infected. We must perform our due diligence when determining whether the event has been fully removed. This will require us to understand what the root cause of the incident was.

We may have to replay the steps of the incident and look through the timelines and any documentation that was created during the incident to understand the root cause. When understanding the root cause, you and your team may have to get extremely technical or have a third-party vendor come in and assist in performing forensic analysis on the IT resources.

Remediating the cause of the infection is also a requirement before moving systems back into production. If an adversary took advantage of a vulnerability, track down the vulnerability and make sure that no other systems are susceptible to that issue. If someone took advantage of an open port on a server, re-evaluate whether that port or service needs to be opened to the public internet.

We also need to verify that our restoration efforts are successful. This can encompass ensuring that systems are restored appropriately and we have validated that the information is not corrupted. Backup systems have automated means of checking the validity of the information being restored, but you may also want to verify that yourself manually. Create snapshots of systems and attempt to restore them in an isolated environment to test the backup and restoration process.

RC.RP-06

The criteria for determining the end of incident recovery are applied, and incident-related documentation is completed.

Your policies and procedures should help you determine when an incident has subsided and the incident can be closed out. Once this has occurred, you can then decide to close out the recovery phase and begin your lessons learned or **after-action review** (**AAR**). This is the final step in the incident response and recovery process.

The lessons learned or AAR should be a required step in the process of your incident response plan. This AAR process is meant to help you, your team, and the business become more efficient when it comes to incident response and recovery. The AAR will capture what went right, what went wrong, and steps to improve the process altogether.

The AAR will help streamline the process of becoming better for your response to an incident. We can ask questions such as, *What could we have done better to improve the process?* or *Were the appropriate steps taken to remediate the incident?* We can use the answers to review our internal processes and adjust them to do better next time.

The process of running an AAR should occur after every incident too. This will again help us do better at responding to an incident. It can have other benefits as well, such as increasing the level of maturity of our response and recovery efforts.

After we have successfully completed our restoration task and concluded our AAR, we can successfully close out the incident. The incident report should be stored in a safe location. We also want to implement separation of duties of the report as it will contain sensitive information that could put the organization in danger if it were to fall into the wrong hands.

Incident recovery communication (RC.CO)

In this section, we will take a look at how we communicate our recovery to internal and external stakeholders. We will need to have plans in place for what we communicate and to whom. There are regulatory requirements that we must follow as well and we must ensure that we follow those guidelines so that we do not fall out of compliance.

RC.CO-03

> *Recovery activities and progress in restoring operational capabilities are communicated to designated internal and external stakeholders.*

To meet the objectives of this control, we will need to review our contracts and compliance requirements that we have with our trusted third parties. This will require us to utilize our **crisis communication plan** (**CCP**) when communicating our recovery activities while reinforcing that we have our company's and our customers' best intentions at heart.

First, we need a way to securely share this information with others. While our immediate thought will probably be *let's encrypt it!* we need to take a risk-based approach. What we disclose to the ELT may be different than what we share with our customers. Disclosing too much information publicly can be harmful to your business and your trusted third-party vendors.

However, when disclosing highly sensitive information, then yes, it should be encrypted. In addition to encrypting, you should take a least-privileged approach when deciding the audience of the disclosed information. Again, what you disclose to internal team members or the executive team may be different than what is released for public consumption. Utilize the policies and procedures around your CCP to make sure that the right information is going to the correct group of people.

The **traffic light protocol** (**TLP**), created by `first.org`, can help with developing the standards for what to communicate. The TLP is as follows:

- **TLP: RED** – For individuals only; no further disclosure is allowed
- **TLP: AMBER** – Can share information on a need-to-know basis within the organization and with clients
  - **TLP: AMBER+STRICT** – Same as TLP: AMBER but information is only shared within the organization
- **TLP: GREEN** – Can share information within their community or organization
- **TLP: CLEAR** – Information is considered public

You will want to ensure that you keep the ELT updated as much as possible so they can make the necessary decisions when needed. If roadblocks come up, they will be the ones that will assist in removing them. You need to make sure that project status is being communicated as well.

Review contracts between your vendors and customers. It is more than likely that there are communication requirements that you must adhere to. Be sure to review those requirements and place them in a spreadsheet or database to keep track of their breach notification and recovery communications guidelines.

RC.CO-04

Public updates on incident recovery are shared using approved methods and messaging.

You will be required to have a breach notification process in place to meet this control. It will need to detail everything from the response to the recovery of the incident. It will also need to detail how the organization intends to prevent a similar incident from occurring in the future.

When discussing the Response function, we mentioned the need to gather as much information as possible – information about not only the incident but also the metadata. Gathering this level of information is necessary to not only recreate the incident but also get to the root cause. This will help to identify similar incidents in the future and also reduce the response time.

The information gathered during the response and recovery phases will help when determining the root cause of the incident. When determining the root cause, ensure that you have all the necessary information and keep track of those involved in the incident when beginning your investigation. During the investigation, evaluate the information collected and ask questions of those involved to determine where the incident occurred.

The root cause of the incident can come from several different scenarios. These can include vulnerabilities or weaknesses in an IT resource, misconfiguration, or social engineering. Once the root cause has been identified, work on possible solutions to prevent the incident from occurring again, or at least minimize the impact of it.

Once the root cause has been determined and mitigations are in place, we will need to communicate this to stakeholders. This can include the ELT, co-workers, customers, and third parties – this should be outlined in your CCP. In addition to this, ensure that you are following your breach notification requirements for customer and regulatory compliance requirements.

Summary

In this chapter, we discussed the steps that you need to take to recover from an incident. This included information gathering, communications, and root cause analysis. We should have policies and procedures written to determine what to communicate and when we should communicate it. We also need to understand our audience and the information that is being communicated.

We need to gather information on the steps taken to recover from an incident. Much like we did when discussing the Response function with gathering information for putting together a timeline, we need to take similar steps when collecting information for the recovery. Be as detailed as possible. We want to have the ability to recreate an incident if needed through our documentation.

We will need a CCP for what we communicate and with whom. Different audiences will require different types of communication and information to be divulged. For example, you may have been subjected to a compromise of a third-party vendor who provides services to you. You may disclose information about who the third party was to the ELT but you may not want to disclose that information to the public. This is to protect that third party from being targeted in subsequent attacks.

You should also work on obtaining as much information about the event as you can to help you determine the root cause. This will come in handy when working with future events that may be similar in nature. For instance, an employee has fallen victim to an account takeover. When determining the root cause, it is discovered that the incident originated from a social engineering attack. Now you can focus on elevating your security parameters around secure email and user awareness.

Lastly, review your contracts and regulatory requirements around notifications. Chances are you have an external requirement for communicating that you have had an incident within so many days. Be sure to review those requirements so that you do not fail to meet compliance.

That is it; this is the last of the NIST CSF functions. Over the next few chapters, we will discuss how to deal with cybersecurity risk, policies, and standards, and how to perform an assessment.

Part 3:
Applying the Framework

In *Part 3*, we will learn how to apply the six functions by developing policies, standards, and procedures and reducing risk. To better understand our environment, we also need to perform an assessment. This assessment is meant to determine what our current environment looks like and what our future state will be.

This part has the following chapters:

- *Chapter 9, How to Deal with Cyber Risk*
- *Chapter 10, Policies, Standards, and Procedures*
- *Chapter 11, Assessment*

How to Deal with Cyber Risk

Now that we have gotten past all the CSF functions, let us focus on how to deal with cyber risk. The NIST CSF provides the guidance that is needed to align yourself with best practices. It does this through the use of documentation, development of SLAs, responsibilities matrices, and communication. All of this is considered part of administrative control.

The administrative controls provided by the CSF are meant to drive down organizational cyber risk. They do not speak to the responsibilities of risk management, as in who is ultimately responsible for it. We have discussed risk, evaluated our administrative controls, and implemented policies. These are all meant to reduce risk; however, the *who* is still a little unclear.

You may say that the **Chief Information Security Officer (CISO)** is responsible for all cyber risks. Is that right? Does it go to the CISO's boss, who might be the **Chief Information Officer (CIO)** or possibly the **Chief Financial Officer (CFO)**? Who has the ultimate authority? In many cases, the CISO is just an advisor to the executive leadership team and the **Board of Directors (BoD)** in relation to cyber risk. This would make them responsible for accepting the risk overall, but how do we get there?

In this chapter, we will cover the NIST **Risk Management Framework (RMF)**. It encompasses a document from FIPS along with several NIST **Special Publications (SPs)**, such as the following:

- **FIPS 199** – Standards for Security Categorization of Federal Information and Information Systems
- **SP 800-37** – Risk Management Framework for Information Systems and Organizations
- **SP 800-39** – Managing Information Security Risk

While there are plenty of other SPs that cover risk, there are three that we will dive into in this chapter. These documents are meant to develop an organizational structure for your overall risk management program.

This is a program, much like cybersecurity is a program. It cannot be a one-time thing or a set-it-and-forget-it type of process. It needs to be cared for and fed to be anywhere near as effective as it should be. In this chapter, we will cover these three main topics:

- Exploring IT risks

- NIST RMF

- How to apply risk management to IT resources

Now that we know what we will be getting ourselves into, let's get started!

Exploring IT risks

We all experience some type of risk each and every day. You woke up this morning, good job! Made breakfast, wait – was the milk spoiled? Drank your coffee – hope it was not hot enough for you to burn yourself. Then you grabbed the keys and jumped in the car and made it just before 8 AM to clock in on time. How did you get there? Did you speed? Did someone cut you off? Instead of taking the car, I guess you could have ridden the bus or taken the train. Wait, you still could have gotten into an accident.

You see, you took a risk by even getting out of bed this morning. You could have drunk spoiled milk, sipped scorching hot coffee, or sped to get to work on time. These risks are all second nature and you probably don't even think about them. They seem common; it's almost like you're numb to the fact that almost everything can be dangerous.

We can sometimes take the same stance when it comes to cyber risk. There are so many dangers when it comes to IT-based systems, you may feel like you want to encase your systems in concrete and drop them in the middle of the ocean, also no network cables! Taking this stance, however, could spell the need for you to find a new job because no one would be able to do their work.

Cyber risk can sometimes feel subjective, and it is. One company's view of cyber risk is not the same as the next. They could be two separate companies, in the same town, performing the same function, with the same market cap, and still have two differing views of cyber risk. Decentralized IT teams make this even worse by having completely different views of risk while working for the same company. Why is that? Experience? How much money is the company willing to spend on risk reduction? Will the organization supply you with enough personnel to perform all that is necessary?

Let us start with how we evaluate risk. Would you spend $100 to protect $50? No. On the flip side, would you spend $50 to protect $100? Possibly. There are several factors that should be considered for the asset, such as its age or its ability to be upgraded. While these are just examples, they tell us how much we may value an asset and the information that resides on it. Just because the value of the asset may be $100 does not mean the value of the information on the asset is not worth way more than that. Now that we know that how we deal with risk is completely different, how about we take a closer look?

There are four primary ways that we deal with risk, all of which are meant to perform a task when risk is identified:

- **Mitigate**: This is where we do something about the risk. It quite possibly could be as simple as applying a software patch or buying new firewalls for the network. It could also be retiring a legacy system.

- **Transfer**: We are transferring the risk to a different party. We mostly think of risk transfer as purchasing a cyber insurance policy. Transferring could also mean that we transfer the security of our network to a third party such as AWS or Microsoft Azure.

- **Avoid**: Avoiding risk involves scrapping the project because the risk is just too high. You have a legacy system in your environment; instead of mitigating the risk, you decide to move the legacy system out of production. This could also mean that you do not take on a project due to its high risk.

- **Accept**: This is typically the last way to deal with risk because it could open you up to significant issues. With acceptance, you do not plan to put any mitigations in place, you do not plan to transfer the risk to an insurance company, and you cannot avoid it. In this case, you ultimately accept the risk. This can lead to a compromised system, so move forward with caution.

These are the four main ways to deal with risk, but that does not tell us about where risk begins or who is responsible for it. In this next section, we will discuss the three tiers of cyber risk.

NIST RMF

The NIST RMF takes a simplistic approach to evaluating cyber risk throughout the organization. At the top of the triangle, we start off with tier 1, which is primarily made up of the BoD and the **Executive Leadership Teams** (**ELTs**). They are responsible for defining the risk and its thresholds. When it comes to tier 2, we take the definitions and place them into policies, standards, and procedures. These are then pushed by the enterprise architecture team to define the standards to be used by the organization. Lastly, tier 3 is the tier where the IT systems reside:

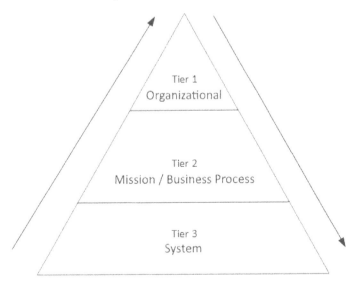

Figure 9.1 – NIST SP 800-37 RMF

Tier 1

Organizational risk is first defined by the BoD and ELTs. They are the ones that state what their level of risk or their risk tolerance is. Back when I said cyber risk can be subjective, this is what I meant. There is no standard definition that states that you must patch a vulnerability within one day, nor is there a regulation that states that you must be protected by cyber insurance as is the case for car insurance.

It is subjective in that they tell the company what should and should not be done based on experience and what they feel is in the best interests of the company. It is up to you, as the cyber professional, to ensure that the risk of doing (or even not doing) a particular task will cost the company. The company could state that a secure email gateway is just not in the budgets for this year. While you have expressed your concerns about not having one, it is ultimately their decision. Now it is up to you to still ensure that email is protected with the tools that you have.

Tier 2

Throughout the chapters that covered the NIST CSF functions, we discussed documentation. Tier 2 is where that documentation is created and enforced. Tier 1 is where the organizational risk is defined. Now we can take those definitions and put them down on paper. In the next chapter, we will discuss how to create a **Policy, Standard, and Procedure (PSP)** framework, but in this chapter, we will briefly discuss what that means.

A policy is a statement document that shows intent. These documents are meant to be high-level in that you can freely hand them out to your friends, family, and loved ones and not feel like you are giving away the keys to the kingdom. For example, a policy document could state that all hard drives shall be encrypted; great! However, the policy document should not state how that encryption is being performed or what the encryption algorithm being used is, nor should it state where the keys should be stored. That is where standards and procedures come in.

The **Enterprise Architecture (EA)** team is responsible for establishing standards. EA takes the requirements from tier 1 and implements those in the environment. In addition to implementing standards, they are responsible for writing up standards documents. For example, the BoD and ELT state that there needs to be additional focus on preventing attacks from the internet. The current set of firewalls only block source/\destination/port/and protocol, which was fine in its day, but the organization needs better protection. To prevent new attacks from coming into the network, EA decides that there need to be IDS/IPS capabilities.

The organization has already deployed a set of firewalls and standardized on a given manufacturer. Now, implementing the IDS/IPS configuration will require an evaluation of the current set and whether the functionality can be utilized. If it cannot, then you will need to begin looking at different hardware. While you may have standardized on Cisco in the past, the new firewalls may be from Cisco again, or a different brand. The point is that once a set of firewalls has been chosen, the EA's responsibility is to ensure that this new brand is used throughout the organization.

The cost of training and being an SME on one set of firewalls can be high. Being an SME for multiple firewall manufacturers could greatly increase this cost even further. This is why standards are so important. I have seen decentralized IT teams that were so siloed that it more than tripled the cost of deployments. One example is when I spoke with an organization that had one set of switches for data, another set of switches for voice, and yet another set of switches for wireless. All of these switches were supplied by different manufacturers utilizing different technologies. Could you imagine the cost savings that would come with having everything contained within one product?

Tier 3

Tier 3 requires a review of risk at the IT resource level. This will include those who are responsible for the engineering of IT systems and keeping the lights on. Risks associated with tier 3 typically involve evaluating and monitoring the cyber risk of the environment. For example, a SOC analyst may be responsible for reviewing the vulnerabilities in a given system and evaluating how to remediate them. They may also be responsible for ensuring that the vulnerability scans are performed at predetermined intervals to ensure that adequate protection is provided.

Tier 3 is also responsible for taking the requirements documents provided by the EA and ensuring that they are implemented and configured appropriately. If the EA states that the IDS/IPS should have the following signatures configured and places the IPS in blocking mode, it is the responsibility of the engineering team to ensure that it is implemented appropriately. Tier 3 also performs the following functions:

- **Prepare**: Prepare to execute the RMF at the organizational and system level
- **Categorize**: Ensure that you have categorized the system and information
- **Select**: The initial set of controls used to secure the environment
- **Implement**: Implement the controls
- **Assess**: Ensure that the controls are working as intended
- **Authorize**: An authorizing official has signed off on the project so that it can move forward
- **Monitor**: Monitor the controls that were implemented ensuring they work as intended

The importance of the tiering shown in *Figure 9.1* is that while requirements are pushed down from tier 1 to subsequent tiers, it also has the ability to flow upward from tier 3 to tier 2, and finally to the organizational tier. It is important to note that since requirements flow downward, issues must flow upward. Why? If you continually push downward, how will you know whether those requirements are working as intended? There must be a continual loop built into the process.

Risk management framework

We briefly discussed the framework steps in our discussion of the responsibilities of tier 3. Now let us put those steps into practice. The following steps are used when evaluating an IT system, or environment, and ensuring that it has adequate controls implemented.

Prepare

This is where we gather the requirements for the project. Is the system going to be used for just our website or will credit cards flow through it? Will it store ePHI or intellectual property? All of these questions should be well thought out before you embark on standing up the system. It will end up costing you more in the long run if you do not properly plan for the company's (and regulatory) requirements.

Categorize

Once we have prepared all of our requirements, we need to categorize the system. To do this, we will use the **Confidentiality, Integrity, and Availability (CIA)** triad. The CIA acronym stands for the following:

- **Confidentiality**: Protecting the information from those who should not have access to it
- **Integrity**: Ensuring that the information has not been altered in any way
- **Availability**: Maintaining uptime for those who are responsible for the documents

We will now use FIPS 199 to determine the watermarks for thresholds for the CIA triad. The watermarks include low-, moderate-, and high-risk categorizations and are determined by the following criteria.

Low

A watermark of low pertains to the CIA triad as having little to no impact on the organization. Loss of systems or monetary value has little impact on the organization's bottom line. Cyber threats are reconnaissance in nature and pose no threat to the overall stability of the network.

Examples include the following:

- Loss of a server in a highly available cluster
- Ping sweeps
- SPAM email received by one person

Moderate

A moderate watermark indication could have a significant impact on the organization and its overall functionality. A moderate loss in CIA can lead to a significant loss of monetary value, the loss of a high-impact system, or the theft of intellectual property. A moderate impact could greatly affect a system's ability to function at normal levels and run in a degraded state for long periods of time.

Examples include the following:

- A virus outbreak affecting multiple systems

- A tier 1 system that is down for long periods of time

- Phishing email resulting in an account takeover

- The transferral of funds

High

The high watermark is reserved for those incidents that are considered catastrophic to the business. A catastrophic event could be that the entire data center is down or that a ransomware event took place. It can also mean the loss of human life because of failure. Computer systems that pertain to hospitals and law enforcement will contain high watermarks due to the nature of their job responsibilities.

Examples include the following:

- Ransomware attacks

- Attacks against medical facilities

- Losses of funds that could result in a material finding

Calculating the security categorization

Now that we have defined our categorization watermarks, let us put them to use. There are plenty of ways to calculate the cyber risk of an asset. Many of us in the profession are used to the following calculation:

*Risk == Threat * Likelihood * Impact*

This is heavily used in cybersecurity textbooks as a way to provide a quantitative calculation of risk that pertains to an IT resource. This was used to evaluate risk and define which systems had the highest impact on the risk calculation. The security categorization provided by *NIST FIPS 199* is used to evaluate the risk using qualitative means.

We only showed low-, moderate-, and high-risk watermarks in the previous section. One thing to note is that you can also have **Not Applicable (N/A)** as a watermark. You see, IT resources cannot have N/A as a watermark. Why? They must maintain a level of confidentiality, integrity, and availability. Data, on the other hand, can have an N/A watermark due to its public nature. If, for instance, you have a public-facing website that has, you guessed it, public information, would it be considered low? Not really. Low means that there is still some level of scrutiny on the data itself. If it is public, do we really care? If the web server that is presenting the public information were compromised, would we care about the data? No, because it was public. What we do care about, however, is the fact that the server was compromised and could potentially present misleading information that impairs our ability to maintain credibility.

The security categorization formula is as follows:

SC data/IT resource == {(confidentiality, impact), (integrity, impact), (availability, impact)}

How do we break this down? The output on the left is the result of the calculations on the right of the equals sign. For example, we have a public web server that presents publicly available information. The calculation of the IT resource would be as follows:

SC web server == {(confidentiality, low), (integrity, low), (availability, moderate)}

Web server == moderate

Now that we have defined the values that go into each impact, how do we perform the calculation? This is the easy part! We take the highest watermark that is applied and use that as our security categorization. In this instance, the security categorization for the web server would be considered moderate.

We can also do this for the information that resides on the IT resource. The next example is for publicly available information:

SC public data == {(confidentiality, N/A), (integrity, low), (availability, low)}

Public data == low

Select

Now that we have categorized our data and the IT resources that house it, we must select the controls to secure the system. Typically, this is reserved for us to align the security categorization to another cybersecurity framework – NIST SP 800-53. NIST SP 800-53 is a massive cybersecurity framework used mostly by federal and state governments. This control framework is made up of thousands of controls that span 20 control families. While we are focusing on the NIST CSF, it is important to know that the CSF is not the only framework they develop. If you want to see how the CSF and SP 800-53 align, look no further than the information references found in the CSF. Most of the controls come from SP 800-53.

You also have the ability to select your own controls when protecting an IT resource. Maybe you have common controls such as **Active Directory Directory Services** (**AD DS**) or a common **Endpoint Detection and Response** (**EDR**) platform. Common controls provide security for several or possibly all of your IT infrastructure. It is important to know that the common controls you implement also meet the regulatory requirements.

Implement

Now that we have prepared our environment, categorized the infrastructure, and selected our security controls, it is time to implement the controls. Implementing controls can come in many forms. It could involve only putting in controls to mitigate cyber risks, just as it could also mean implementing a workflow for transferring the risk to another third party. Implementing is not just for configuring the controls; we also need to evaluate the risks associated with the implementation of that particular control.

Implementation also does not mean that you must manually place every single control on a given system. You can also do this through automated means. Microsoft Windows-based shops will more than likely use Active Directory's **Group Policy Objects** (**GPOs**) to push security configurations to the entire environment. Linux/UNIX-based environments may use automated tools such as Ansible to push down configurations. The point is that you must implement the controls that were selected from the previous phase.

Assess

We now verify that the environment has been set up as intended. This validation is necessary to ensure that the proper security controls have been implemented. There also needs to be a way to check that the necessary configurations have been made and that they stay that way. This means that if you detect drift, then you must have a way to correct it.

The *assess* phase of the RMF is used to validate the configurations are implemented, as set out by EA. EA will collect all the necessary policies and standards, including any regulatory requirements. When making the configurations, it is important that these are covered during the design phase of the **System Development Life Cycle** (**SDLC**).

Collecting configuration drift information can be tricky, which is why I suggest using an automated configuration service. Puppet is a service that can detect such drift information and correct it automatically. Other services such as Terraform and **Infrastructure as Code** (**IaC**) can also detect certain types of drift and can correct it when necessary.

We should also assess the common controls that have been implemented in a system environment. Common controls are those that are commonly used across the environment such as AV or **Identity and Access Management** (**IAM**). These controls may have been set up originally with little to no control mechanisms in mind. You must assess these controls to ensure that they also meet or exceed the company's policies and procedures, as well as any regulatory requirements.

Authorize

Another critical piece of all of this is to authorize the operation of the new system or service. This **Authorization to Operate** (**ATO**) is the last required step before the system is placed into a production environment. It is meant for an authorizing official, typically personnel from the business, to review and approve the system to go to production. A **Systems Security Plan** (**SSP**) is what is needed for the authorizing official to sign off on the security controls.

An SSP is a living document that details the security controls, scope, and risks associated with the new system. This document depicts everything in the environment and provides information so the authorizing official can make a calculated determination of whether the system is productionized.

The details that go into the SSP are crucial to the success of the service. The SSP needs to capture not only the security controls that were implemented but also any risks that are associated with the service. The authorizing official can then decide whether the service, and the risks associated with the service, is acceptable, or whether the risk needs to be transferred or avoided altogether.

Once the determination has been made for the system to go to production, the authorizing official signs off on the risk, which gives the go-ahead to operate the new system. The SSP shall have the signatures from the authorizing official stating that the business has accepted the risks associated with the service.

Monitor

Lastly, we monitor the service to ensure its success. We can monitor the system in several different ways. For example, we need to monitor the common controls associated with the service. This includes ensuring that antivirus definitions are updated accordingly, or user access is reviewed. We need to monitor configuration drift to ensure that we have a standardized environment. Monitoring shall also include SNMP to determine the overall health of the systems and the environment.

Most importantly, we need to monitor the overall health and security of the service. While automated means help when resources are thin, you should also periodically perform manual scans to ensure that automated means are configured appropriately. Automation is great and should be incorporated within the environment. However, it should also be monitored. Automation does fail from time to time and until you audit the automation, you could have a false sense of security.

How to apply risk management to IT resources

The SDLC has similarities to the RMF. One topic of discussion when it comes to the SDLC and the RMF is identifying cyber risks associated with IT resources. When identifying risks, it is a necessity to record them in a document that is also presented to the authorizing official.

A critical component of the SSP is the risk register. This risk register is where all identified risks are recorded and then placed into a project plan for remediation. As we assess the IT resources, we identify risks associated with the environment. We then evaluate how we want to resolve these risks, whether that means accepting, avoiding, mitigating, or transferring them. If we decide to mitigate or transfer the risks, a **Plan of Action and Milestones (POA&M)** shall be created to record the progress of remediation.

The POA&M is a project plan used to track remediation efforts. The POA&M should include the following:

- Risk ID

- Description of the risk

- How long it will take to complete the remediation

- Resources involved, such as personnel, time, and cost

- Priority of the remediation task(s)

- Identifying the system that alerted personnel to the risk

- Who is responsible for the remediation task(s)

- Risks of not remediating the vulnerability

- Start and end dates

An additional topic of discussion is how we deal with the IT resource once it has reached the end of its life.

End-of-life resources, and how you deal with the associated risks, will be important. Many times, we just perform a backup of all the information and then get rid of the hardware. Careful consideration is needed when deciding what to do with the information that was backed up. For example, if we dispose of our hardware without wiping the drives first, and there is sensitive information on the drives, this could be considered a material breach. Why? The answer is simple: it is trivial to extract a hard drive from one machine and mount it to another machine.

We must ensure that we dispose of the information securely. This includes using encryption at the drive level, or whatever mechanism is available for your backups. Securely wiping the drive once it has been backed up will also be required. You want to ensure that all information that was stored on the drive has been expunged to the best of your ability.

We previously mentioned that the SSP is a living document that details the IT resources and the environment. The SSP should reflect how an IT resource was decommissioned from the network. The document should state how the information was backed up from one system to another, how it is safeguarded, where it is stored, and how to retrieve it later in the event that it is needed. Once the system is backed up and shut down for the last time, then it is appropriate to archive the information and place the system's SSP on the shelf for historical purposes.

We also never delete information from the SSP or the risk register. Again, for historical purposes, the SSP should reflect all the effort that you and your team have put into safeguarding the resource. When risks are identified and remediated, they should be marked off the list, but never removed. It is important to know and understand how risks were identified, as well as the actions that were taken to remove each risk from the environment.

Framing risk

Framing risk for the SSP is also a necessity when identifying cyber risks. Framing risk has much to do with what is, and is not, included in the environment. For example, when we perform an evaluation of a three-tiered application, we include the presentation, logic, and data tiers. These three (or more) systems can be single standalone systems, or they can be clustered together. The application may require a firewall or **Web Application Firewall** (**WAF**) to front all incoming connections.

It is important to understand how you frame the environment to ensure that the SSP correctly identifies all of the systems and their components. *Figure 9.2* will help clarify this:

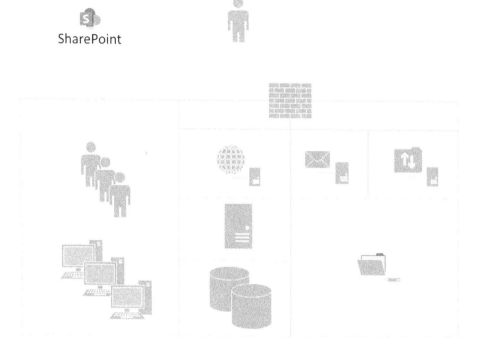

Figure 9.2 – Framing risk

Figure 9.2 shows a typical small business environment; we have employees and their desktops on the left and the server environment on the right. It also shows the use of cloud-based services such as SharePoint. The on-premise environment is protected by a firewall and provides services such as email, FTP, and file and print services. In the middle, we show a three-tiered environment used for credit card transactions.

When we create the SSP for the credit card environment, we will require the documentation to cover the web server, logic, and database. This leaves out the FTP, email, and file and print. However, we would require an SSP for those environments too. The SSP will discuss the security controls of those systems, their configurations, and how they work together to provide services to our employees and customers.

The SSP for file and print should include the types of sensitive information that could reside on the server itself. It should include who has access to the file and print server, as well as the common controls that are used to enforce security policies. The SSP should also discuss how it is being audited and logged to ensure compliance with corporate policies and standards, along with regulatory requirements. It also needs to show how people gain access to the file and print server. Do external employees only have access to it internally or can they also access it through a VPN connection? Once this information has been obtained, we can secure it even further as we have identified the risks involved. This is just a sneak peek at the information that will be covered in *Chapter 10*.

Summary

In this chapter, we learned that identifying and remediating risks is just a single component of the overall approach to cyber risk. We need to have the entire company involved when deciding whether to accept, avoid, mitigate, or transfer cyber risk. Evaluation and dealing with risk come from the top and push downward through the organization.

We also saw how evaluation of cyber risk must first be established by the ELT and BoD. They are the ones that must state what their risk tolerance levels are. Once these have been defined, EA will develop the policies and procedures ensuring that new or existing IT resources are architected in a manner that reflects the acceptable security posture required by the organization.

We learned that it is important to ensure that there is a feedback loop in the event that a particular control is not implemented as intended. This could be a one-off configuration error, or it could be more catastrophic in nature. This leads to unrealized cyber risks in the environment, possibly lending a false sense of security. If a control is not sufficient, it must be flagged to EA and the ELT as soon as possible so the organization can understand it and plan accordingly.

As we saw, it is also important to develop an SSP, or a living document used to show how the environment was set up. The SSP must include all the configuration information about the environment, associated risks, and how IT plans to remediate those risks. Once the documentation is finalized, and the system is ready to be placed into production, it then requires official sign-off from the authorizing official who provides the ATO.

In the next chapter, we will discuss the need for policies, standards, and procedures. These documents are necessary to fulfill several different requirements, including teaching staff what is and is not an appropriate use of technology, as well as auditing requirements.

Policies, Standards, and Procedures

The objective of the NIST CSF is to reduce the overall cyber risk for an organization. We reviewed the six functions of the CSF Coreand the NIST RMF in the last chapter. While we may think that the CSF is only meant for IT risk, it is also meant to reduce organizational risk. The RMF reflects this by going deep into the structure of organizational cyber risk.

The NIST RMF consists of several NIST **Special Publications** (**SP**) and the **Federal Information Processing Standard** (**FIPS**). This series of documents helps organizations to create cybersecurity programs that encompass risk reduction, incident response, and research. In this instance, we specifically looked at SP 800-37, SP 800-39, and FIPS 199. With these in mind, we learned how to implement, or at least start, a risk management program.

In this chapter, we will look at the development and enforcement of policies, standards, and procedures. **Policies, Standards, and Procedures** (**PSP**) are probably the least exciting thing in the world. You will never see a movie produced with someone portraying a CISO writing policies. They are, however, a necessity as they carry out an important function. PSPs drive your administrative controls.

This chapter will cover what policies, standards, and procedures are and their functions. We will create a document structure to make it easy to find what you are looking for. Lastly, there will be a discussion around the approval process in getting the documents signed and approved by executive management. This chapter will cover the following topics:

- The importance of governance
- Framework structure
- Policies
- Standards
- Procedures
- Policy approval

Let's get started!

The importance of governance

Governance is used to set the direction of the company and how it operates. It establishes a functional way that your employees, and your company, operate. Governance is not an easy task by any means. Employees tend to get into a routine and do not look to make changes to that routine. Governance can impede how an employee performs their job functions or can direct an entire organization toward a common goal.

Organizational governance, much like organizational risk management, comes from the top and is pushed down throughout the organization. The board of directors and executive leadership set the direction of governance throughout the organization. It is then your responsibility to take those requirements and apply them to some type of policy. Remember, however, there must be a continual feedback loop that allows analysts and engineers to report failures and present them to top management for review.

While technical controls present many benefits for controlling risk management, administrative controls state the *intent*, the *what*, and the *how* of implementing those technical controls. Control frameworks, including the NIST CSF, require that every technical control is backed up by some type of administrative control. Other regulatory frameworks, including PCI-DSS, also require that you have a policy or standard written for every control you have.

For example, during an audit, the assessor asks to look at a common control, such as vulnerability management. The engineer states that vulnerabilities on IT resources are updated daily and can show the configuration settings that back that up. While this is great and all, it is only part of the overall picture. To be effective, you must have properly written documentation to back up that control setting. This is much more involved than just taking a screenshot of a control setting and considering that good enough.

Governance and administrative controls cannot be developed in a vacuum either. Administrative controls are only as good as their backing by the ELT. For example, you could have written thirty policy documents (containing policies, standards, and procedures) but none of them are enforceable due to the fact that they were never approved by management. There must be an approval workflow in addition to their development.

There should be a governance structure and workflow for how policy documents are approved. This will provide the enforcement needed when a policy document is not followed. There must be consequences for not following the policy document as intended. However, there is no standard way of stating what those consequences shall be; that is left up to management to decide.

The next couple of sections will discuss policy governance, how policies are approved, and structure.

Policy workflow

Our first example is the policy workflow and executive sign-off for any policy document that is written, as follows:

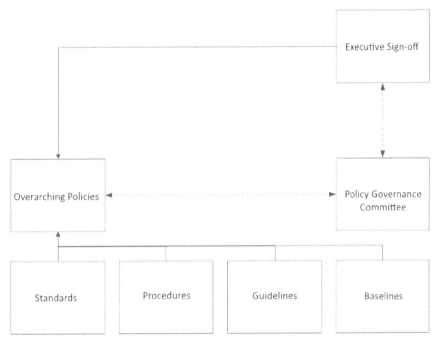

Figure 10.1 – Policy workflow

Figure 10.1 depicts a standard policy workflow. When developing policy documents, remember that they should flow up to the overarching policies that were written. This includes standards, procedures, guidelines, and baselines. As they align with the policy (more on this later), they are then reviewed by a policy governance committee. This committee shall be the preliminary group responsible for the review and approval of any policy documents being developed. The committee, however, is not responsible for signing off on the execution of the document as this is reserved for executive management. Remember, risk mitigation and response come from the top down and must be enforced by an executive or a team of executives.

Executive Sign-off has an arrow coming down to overarching policies as well. This is to state that the ELT shall influence the decisions made by the policy. The policy shall influence the standards, and so on. The two-way arrows between the policies and the committee show that the policies could be sent back for re-work to ensure that they meet the overall objectives stated by the ELT. This goes for the policy committee and executive sign-off as well. Both the committee and the ELT can veto the sign-off until the document complies with business objectives.

Policy creation

Regardless of whether the policy document is new, or it already exists, it always starts off as a draft. The policy shall be drafted and then presented to the policy governance committee. This committee is responsible for the review and approval of the draft policy document. Once all members have approved the draft policy document, it then shall be reviewed and approved by your ELT. Once this has been approved, the policy document must reside in some type of document repository, whether that is Microsoft SharePoint or Atlassian's Confluence. It must be presented so that all employees have permission to read the policy.

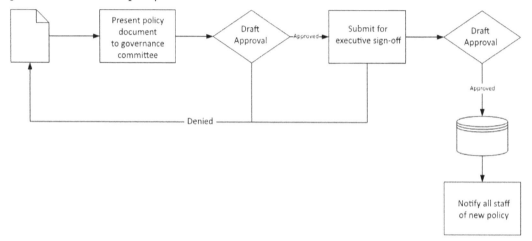

Figure 10.2 – New policy development

If at any time the document is denied, it must go all the way back to draft format and be edited so that it will meet business objectives. Once the document meets those requirements, it must go through the same process of being reviewed by the governance committee and then to the executive again for review and approval.

Reviewing policies and procedures

Each policy document should have a review cycle as well. These review cycles typically occur annually; however, they should not be more than two years. Review cycles are necessary to review and potentially update the documentation based on new standards that have been released since it was last reviewed.

Each document should have a footer that states when the last update to the document was approved by the executive management and when the next update should occur. This is all part of the document lifecycle management that must occur to ensure that the documents align with the business objectives stated in the document:

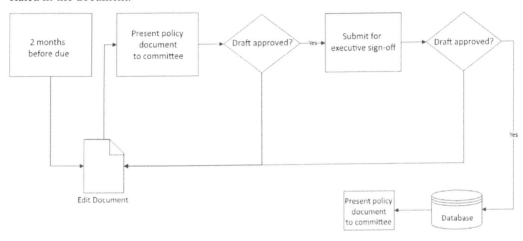

Figure 10.3 – Policy review cycle

We shall use the approval date as a guide for when the policy is ready to go through its review cycle. We kick off the review a few months in advance of its renewal date to ensure that it gets approved before it expires. Much like new policies, policy reviews occur at least every 2 years, if not sooner. When reviewing the policy document, ensure that it flows to the governance committee and then to an executive for official sign-off. Once complete, the draft will go back into the database repository for everyone to review. Lastly, do not forget to send out a notification to all staff members that the new policy documents exist for them to review as well.

Policy review and approval is crucial to the overall success of the program. Without having a periodic review process, your documents could become stale and unusable for auditing purposes. Ensure that you are following some type of cycle for all policies being created.

Framework structure

There must be a structured format when creating policies; otherwise, how would you know what you are looking for? The structure does not have to be difficult to implement, nor are we implementing the Dewey Decimal System. However, there should be a method to your madness.

As we look at the overall structure of how the policies, standards, and procedures should be laid out, it is important to know what goes into the document too. Policies should be high-level documents stating the intent for a task, or its *why*. Standards are mid- to low-level documents stating the *what*. Procedures should state *how* something is to be configured. If our objective is to be high level, then what is the point of writing the document? Third-party assessors, or your strategic partners, may want to view what is in your policies. The intention is to have the ability to share information without the need for a **Non-Disclosure Agreement (NDA)**. In fact, you should write your policies in such a way that you can post them on your public website without fear of giving away too much information.

You will need to have a structure in place so that you can easily find what you are looking for in a policy document. *Figure 10.4* depicts how you could structure your policy documents:

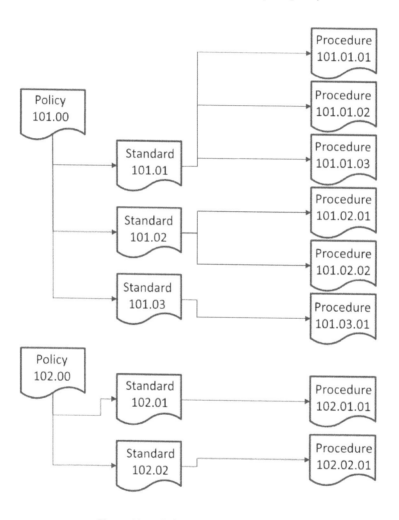

Figure 10.4 – Policy document framework

Policy structure is important, especially when you have numerous policy documents that you must manage. As previously mentioned, policies are high-level documents that state the intent behind a particular task. These documents can be shared with second and third parties without the need for the other side to sign an NDA.

Standards back up policies as they state *how* something is to be performed. For example, you may have an encryption standard that lays out the necessary encryption requirements. In this instance, we have decided to only allow the use of the **transport layer security** (**TLS**) version 1.2 or higher. This is because there are issues with anything less than that version of the protocol. You may also want to state which types of hashing algorithms you should use, such as SHA256 instead of MD5.

It is important to note that while policies should be high-level, standards and procedures are not. Due to this, you should require an NDA to be put in place prior to providing this information to anyone outside of the organization. In many cases, standards and procedures state low-level configurations and responses to incidents that, if they fall into the wrong hands, could be detrimental to the organization. Several third parties will have a mutual NDA that can be signed between the two or more parties; however, check with your legal counsel before moving forward.

Standards are highly important as they state *what* needs to be configured, whom you do business with, or how to respond to an incident. A standard can also be used for the structure of a team or task. You may have an incident response plan in place that states how to structure the team. In the standards, you could put your incident response team call tree or a RACI chart showing responsibilities.

Procedures state *how* to do something, and they back up the standards. In our previous example, we discussed encryption. We stated that anything less than a TLS 1.2 is unacceptable for production use. This is great and all, but how do you configure it? This is where the procedure comes into play. The procedure backs up the standard and says now that we have determined TLS 1.2 is acceptable, this is how we configure the system to prevent anything less than that from working on a production system.

Think of each number associated with the policies, standards, and procedures as a control family. Control family 101 could state how to secure software development, whereas control family 102 could focus on network security. 103 could handle human resources functions, and so on. The point is to break the control families up appropriately enough so that you can easily find exactly what you are looking for.

Each control family is then backed up by a list of standards that were originally stated in the policy. Again, the policy could state that you intend to encrypt hard drives, and the standard discusses the appropriate encryption algorithm to be used when encrypting those hard drives. As an example, you have 100.00 as an encryption control family, which states the intention to encrypt anything and everything. 100.01 states the appropriate encryption algorithms to use. 100.02 states what ciphers are appropriate for TLS connections, while 100.03 states the appropriate database encryption technologies. 100.03.01 states how to implement database encryption technologies in your system. Every database company will do this differently. For instance, an Oracle database may use **transparent database encryption** (**TDE**), while Microsoft SQL Server may use a different technology. These would be split into two separate procedures to get them configured appropriately.

The layout could look like the following:

Policy No	Policy Name	Standard No	Standard Name	Procedure No	Procedure Name
100.00	Encryption				
		100.01	Encryption Algorithms		
		100.02	TLS Encryption		
				100.02.01	Apache
				100.02.02	Microsoft IIS
		100.03	Remote connectivity		
				100.03.01	SSH
				100.03.02	RDP

Table 10.1 – Policy framework layout

This structure is just an example; however, it could be populated with several other topics, such as acceptable use or application security. The documents should all follow the same structure. That way, you can find exactly what you are looking for.

Policies

Organizations all too often will combine a policy with a standard or procedure. This can be troublesome when you are trying to provide the correct information, especially during an audit. A policy is an overarching document that supplies the intent of implementing a control or control family. Policies are high-level documents used to establish governance with the intention of implementing administrative, technical, and physical controls used to reduce organizational risk.

Policies should not go into detail about the configurations or processes that an employee or a piece of technology should use. This is the job of standards and procedures. Policies are high level, meaning that you should write the document in such a way that you are not giving away too much information.

As previously stated, policies state the intent of doing or performing a particular task. For example, if you intend to place smart card readers at each of your ingress/egress points to a building, this should be stated in the policy. This, however, does not mean that you state that you are using a standardized piece of technology to use for card reader access. It should also not go into detail about how it is configured or the levels of encryption being used.

Other topics you would normally see in a policy are vocabulary and responsibilities. You could state in the policy that team members are responsible for the maintenance of a system; however, we do not go into detail about what the type of maintenance is. As an example, a policy could state that the server team is responsible for patch management of all IT systems and services, whereas the network team is responsible for the upkeep of the network equipment.

We do not state when the patches will be made. This is giving too much information away. If an adversary knows that you patch the weekend after Microsoft's patch Tuesday, this means the adversary has a week after the patches are released to attack your infrastructure with known vulnerabilities. Providing this level of detail, without an NDA being in place, will open you up for additional unwanted risk.

Standards

Standards are documents that many of us are familiar with. They are mid- to low-level documents that state the *what* of configurations, settings, and intended outcomes. They are used to describe what is and what is not acceptable from an organizational level. Standards are also used to back up the intent of the policy and provide enough detail for someone to write a procedure for performing that task.

A standards document does not detail how to implement something; that is the job of the procedure. A standard is a document that states what is an acceptable approach to a particular job function or configuration setting. In a previous example, we discussed appropriate configuration settings for encryption. For our 100.02 encryption standard, we could state the following:

- Disable TLS versions 1.1 and lower

- Must use FIPS 140-2 encryption standards

- Keys must be newly generated when a key is issued or re-issued due to expiration

- Asymmetric encryption algorithms:

    - RSA must use a 2,048 – 4,096 bit strength

    - ECDSA must use a 256 – 521 bit strength

- All legacy protocols must be disabled prior to being placed into production

- Wireless networks must use WPA2-PSK or WPA2-Enterprise

As you can see, a standard such as this one would state the appropriate configurations for items on an IT resource. The standard can certainly go into greater detail regarding examples of unacceptable encryption algorithms to be used or the dangers of using legacy protocols.

Care must be taken when creating documentation with this level of detail as it could provide much greater detail than what is intended for public consumption. This is why you should have an NDA in place to safeguard against the exposure of sensitive information. You could make an exception for a web service to allow a weaker protocol to be used, but again, keep this information as close to you as possible.

Standards will also play key roles in how the procedures are developed. More on that in the next section.

Procedures

Writing a procedure is an art. Why? A procedure must be written in such a way that a junior-level analyst can understand how to configure a piece of technology without prior knowledge. Many times when a procedure is written, it leaves out key pieces of information that are needed to configure an IT resource. This can become frustrating to the employee who is required to configure something or fix a problem.

Would your team know how to resolve an issue if you or a senior employee left to go on vacation? The point of writing a procedure is to write it with so much detail that it does not leave anything to question. A procedure should have each and every step discussed to the point that what to do and how to do it is completely unambiguous.

I used to teach Linux classes at a community college, and I thought I had it all planned out. You see, we allowed our students to check out external hard drives for use during the semester. These hard drives were used to install a version of Ubuntu Linux so the students could get used to the software and do their homework assignments. There was only one catch, however; how would the students get Ubuntu on the drive if they had never performed an install before?

I wrote up an assignment that walked through the installation of the operating system onto the external drive. However, there was another catch – which hard drive to install it on once it was booted? For me, it was a given: do not pick the internal hard drive of the desktop. Some of the students understood, while some accidentally installed Ubuntu on the wrong drive.

While this was a learning curve for my students, it was a learning moment for me too. I left out a key step in the process, which was to state the correct drive to install the operating system on. This not only left my students unhappy because they had to do it all over again; it also made IT unhappy because they had to reimage the computer before the next class!

The level of detail that you put into the procedure is highly important. If it requires a reboot, put that in the document. If there is a registry setting that needs to be configured, put that in the document too. Even though you know you have to click the **Next** button 10 times to install a piece of software, state that. Leave nothing to chance. What will happen is that either you will get a call while you are on vacation stating that a system went down and you have to fix it, or someone will misconfigure a setting and that someone may not notice the error until it is too late.

What was stated to be configured in the standard is carried over into the procedure. The procedure walks you through the installation of a system or setting that was defined in the standard. Procedures are meant to back up standards. For example, policy 100.00 stated your intention to encrypt everything. Standard 100.01 is meant to define the appropriate encryption algorithms to use, while 100.02 discusses appropriate TLS configurations. Now, we get to the procedures. 100.02.01 Apache is meant to walk you through how to configure your Apache server for TLS 1.2/1.3, whereas 100.02.02 discusses how to register for the same TLS protocol on Microsoft Server IIS.

Standard 100.03 discusses the appropriate protocols to be used when connecting to a remote computer, while the associated procedures discuss how to configure **secure shell** (**SSH**) (100.03.01) and the **remote desktop protocol** (**RDP**) (100.03.02). This simplifies the breakdown of the documentation by going directly to the source of the information that you are looking for.

Policy document format

The alignment, numbering, and contents of the documents should have a familiar format for every policy document produced. These documents should at the very least contain the following:

- **Purpose**: What is the purpose of the document being produced? What is it meant to establish?

- **Owner**: When tying a policy document to an owner, ensure that it does not follow a particular person's name. The document should reference the position of the person or the department. This is to future-proof the document in the event of turnover or any other type of departmental change.

- **Scope**: What is the overall scope that the document is supposed to cover? Shall it encompass only internal staff or external third parties? Maybe both? Could it also include on-premises or SaaS-based applications?

- **Policy statement**: A policy statement should be clear, concise, and to the point. This is where we state the intent for a particular control (for policies), what or where something should be implemented or configured (for standards), or the process for implementing a control (for procedures).

- **Information references**: This section is not mandatory, but it should be considered as part of your policy documents. The *information references* section should show the alignment of the policy documents with a given framework or frameworks. For example, if you align your policy documents with the NIST CSF, it should state which controls or control families it aligns with. If, for instance, you are writing a policy document that covers incident response, you should have references in the policy document that state which controls this policy document aligns with. If you decide that you also want to include other frameworks, outside of the NIST CSF, you should include them as well.

As previously mentioned, the structure of the policies, standards, and procedures is important. Policies are meant to be high level, allowing anyone to view them without providing too much detail. This is why breaking out standards and procedures is important so that you do not provide highly risky information without an NDA being in place.

Policy control families

Creating your policy framework can be intimidating. *Table 10.1* only shows a small snippet of what should be considered for policy documents, not to mention that the framework should include an exhaustive list of controls when starting out, as you may only have a handful of controls.

There are a few lists that can assist you when starting out creating your own framework. The Open Policy Framework is an open source project aimed at assisting policymakers. It lays out several control families that you can use to start your own framework. These include the following:

- **Information security**: The information security control family is aimed at data protection and acceptable use. Standards documents could include the acceptable use policy, encryption, data disposal, and **information lifecycle management** (**ILM**). The information security control family is meant to control and secure the organization's sensitive information.

- **Asset management**: There is a reason that the Center for Internet Security states that asset management is the most important control. *You cannot protect what you cannot see!* The organization should have sound controls over asset management, including the identification of software and services that also run on the IT resource. If you do not know that the asset or software exists, would you have a game plan to patch or mitigate any risks?

- **Human resources**: This control family is meant to explain what to do with an employee's access and company-owned possessions during their employment. When a new employee is hired, the manager must go through a series of steps to ensure that the new hire has everything they need to do their job functions. This may include receipt of a new computer, a company-owned cell phone, or peripherals.

  When an employee is transferred to a different position, you will need to have standards that explain what to do with those possessions or access to IT resources. You want to ensure that access creep is not introduced into the environment by allowing the employee to have access to the same IT resources they previously had if their new job does not require it.

  We also want to create standards for what to do when the employee is offboarded. What do you do if an employee is let go or leaves freely on their own? This all gets planned out in the offboarding standard that must be written. These standards could also be written in coordination with Human Resources to ensure that both departments are aligned with what is stated in the standard.

- **Physical security**: There are plenty of physical security controls that could be discussed in this section, such as **closed-circuit television** (**CCTV**), physical barriers, man traps, key card door access, and many others. These controls shall have their own control family to be tracked. Several frameworks also mention physical security in their documentation as well. These controls should be depicted in the policy documents that are written for your organization.

- **Access control**: Least privilege and separation of duties, password standards, use of **multifactor authentication** (**MFA**), and identity proofing are controls that fall under access control. Access control is more than just controlling the level of access a user has on a given device. While least privilege and separation of duties are important, there are several other standards that should be developed.

  We should look at developing standards around the types of MFA that are allowed in the environment. For example, several MFA vendors provide differing levels of access, such as push notifications, U2F, **one-time passcodes** (**OTPs**), to even landline callbacks and SMS. Each of these has differing levels of risk associated with their authentication. Some MFA mechanisms have additional risks involved, such as using SMS when there is a fear of SIM swapping or push fatigue when using a mobile application.

- **Incident management**: Incident management can include the Recover and Response functions from the NIST CSF core. Controls should include the creation of your security incident response team, a call tree in the event of an incident, how to perform investigations, documenting the incident, and documenting lessons learned.

  This is also where you would align your IR runbooks with the controls. For example, if you have a response plan for how to overcome an account takeover, you should also have a runbook to assist the procedure and visualize the response.

- **Business continuity/disaster recovery**: We have discussed how to respond to a given incident and how to recover from it. Those policies, standards, and procedures for how to conduct this shall be in this family of controls. Standards that should be included in this family include backup and testing, business continuity planning and testing, transitions to hot or cold sites, and recovery and documentation.

- **Security awareness and training**: You may think that security awareness and training are synonymous with each other; however, they are not. According to NIST, security *awareness* is performed through observation, whereas *training* is more focused on security topics. This is something that is done year-round and not just a project that is set aside for security awareness month.

  Security awareness can be done through banner displays or videos set up on TVs. These are meant to be viewed by staff members passing by. Security training is also meant to highlight cybersecurity; however, it is done through more intense and structured means. Security training is focused on the job role or function rather than being just a high-level banner that is viewed. For example, security awareness would highlight the need for extra scrutiny when interacting with a phishing email, whereas training may be required for email administrators who configure the secure email gateway.

- **Secure network configurations**: This control family is meant to highlight the need for secure network configurations. This should include site-to-site VPN connectivity, client-to-site VPNs, and hardening firewalls or other security appliances, such as IDS/IPS. This also highlights the configurations required for VPN setups. For example, many organizations have moved from split-tunneling client-based VPN connections and moved to full tunnels. If you allow one but forbid the other, this should also be in the standard.

  Secure network configurations should also include firewall configurations. Do you deny all and allow by exception in the rule base? Should the firewalls require MFA for authentication? What protocols are never allowed to come through a firewall? These should all be discussed.

- **Secure configuration and management**: All IT resources and software should be hardened against a standard. There are several standards that highlight the need for hardening a system;

however, the best-known standard is the Center for Internet Security benchmarks documents. Hardening means that you remove or change all default settings and credentials on a system. Remove any unwanted or unused services from the system and ensure that proper security configurations have been performed.

- **Risk management**: We have discussed risk quite a bit throughout the book. We now must take everything that we have learned and apply that to policies and standards. NIST has several documents that cover organizational risk: NIST SP 800-30, 800-37, and 800-39. The International Organization of Standards has also developed ISO 27005, which also introduces strategic ways of dealing with risk.

- **Application security**: Software is becoming increasingly important as technology advances. We have heard phrases such as *the web browser is the new desktop* or Web 3.0. Applications are becoming integrated with everything, thanks to **application programming interfaces (APIs)**, which allow you to communicate directly with the application, to exchanging currencies online, an application is the driving force behind it.

This, however, leads to unexpected risks if you have never had to deal with application security before. You should maintain metrics on the various types of applications being developed, how many API endpoints you have, or the extent of testing for the vulnerabilities. You should also deploy static application or dynamic application security testing (SAST or DAST) to scan for misconfigurations or vulnerabilities. Having robust standards on code reviews should also be part of your policy documents to ensure that this is also being conducted.

If you decide that you want more granularity in your control families, take a look at NIST SP 800-53 as this is another great way to develop your policy document framework. NIST SP 800-53 Rev. 5 has 20 separate control families that provide more in-depth information. These control families are as follows:

ID	Family	ID	Family
AC	Access Control	PE	Physical and Environmental Protection
AT	Awareness and Training	PL	Planning
AU	Audit and Accountability	PM	Program Management
CA	Assessment, Authorization, and Monitoring	PS	Personnel Security
CM	Configuration Management	PT	PII Processing and Transparency
CP	Contingency Planning	RA	Risk Assessment
IA	Identification and Authentication	SA	System and Services Acquisition
IR	Incident Response	SC	System and Communications Protection
MA	Maintenance	SI	System and Information Integrity
MP	Media Protection	SR	Supply Chain Risk Management

Table 10.2 – NIST SP 800-53 control families

As you can see, the Open Policy Framework has a total of 12 control families, whereas NIST SP 800-53 Rev. 5 has 20. This is not to say that one is better than the other. Every organization needs a place to start; it is just a matter of where you are currently and what your strategic objectives are for your policy development.

Summary

In this chapter, we discussed several important topics.. Establishing this framework first will drive the policies, standards, and procedures for the organization. When first creating your framework, ensure that it also aligns with business objectives and best practices. This does not necessarily mean that you must get it right the first time; however, if it is not well thought out initially, it could mean additional re-work later. Policies and standards are truly meant to back up all the hard work that you and your team perform daily. Policy documents are also needed to pass an audit as they state what your intent is for having the technology, and how you intend to configure and use it.

Policies are high-level documents meant to be consumed by the public without the need for an NDA. This is an important distinction between a policy and the other documents. Standards and procedures are meant to be mid- to low-level documents that state how a control is being implemented and why. These documents could also state exceptions for security controls that allow an adversary to better understand how the environment is configured.

Lastly, pick a framework to align your policies against rather than starting from scratch. This can alleviate the stress of trying to come up with your own initial structure for the policy documents. Use The Open Policy Framework or other special publications from NIST to align yourself with.

In the next chapter, we will discuss how to assess your organization. This is important so that you can establish the current and future state of the cybersecurity program.

References

1. The open policy framework: `https://theopenpolicyframework.com`

2. NIST Special Publication 800-53 Rev. 5: `https://nvlpubs.nist.gov/nistpubs/SpecialPublications/NIST.SP.800-53r5.pdf`

11

Assessment

Policies, standards, and procedures are an integral part of your cybersecurity program. These policy documents are used to lay the foundation of how you intend to run your cybersecurity program. From information security to asset management and software development, policies are used to document how you run certain programs for your organization.

Policies are meant to be high-level documents used to describe your intent to implement security controls. These documents should be written in such a way that you can freely distribute them or put them on a public site without fear of giving away too much information. The intent is to be able to distribute the documents without the need for an NDA to be in place between the organization and the customer or third-party vendor.

A **standard** is a document used to describe the *what* of the intent. For example, a standard for encryption should have the appropriate encryption algorithms and bit strengths to be used. This document is also meant to discourage the use of legacy protocols as they may be susceptible to certain weaknesses leading to an attack.

A **procedure** is the *how* of implementing something. It is a set of step-by-step instructions for how to configure a particular technology appropriately. This is important to get right as you may have junior-level analysts who may have never configured the hardware or software before and will need assistance in doing so. The intent is to have the document written in such a way that the analyst can configure it without much help from others.

These documents should be split into different control families and broken apart so that you can freely distribute a policy while needing an NDA for standards and procedures. Auditors will also require that you have documentation created in order to back up the claims made about your configurations of IT resources. This is why having policy documents written for the various aspects of your program is extremely important.

In this last and final chapter, we will discuss performing an assessment of your program. This assessment is meant to help you understand where you are currently at with your cybersecurity program; this is called your **current state**. This is a snapshot in time of everything that your program has to offer. We will then develop our strategic roadmap or future state. This is where we want to take our program. In this chapter, we will discuss the following topics:

- Performing the assessment

- Capturing the current state

- Creating your future roadmap

There is a lot to get to, so let's jump in!

Performing the assessment

There are three different ways an assessment can be performed; these are first-, second-, and third-party assessments. Each of these is distinct in the way they are performed, but they ultimately all get to the same result. These assessments are meant to discover deficiencies in your program. These deficiencies can then be turned into objectives or projects to improve your cybersecurity posture.

First-party assessments

A **first-party assessment** can be a fun and exciting way of getting to know your environment. The first-party assessment is performed by either you, your team, or an internal audit department within your organization. An assessment of this kind can highlight many of the things you are doing right but also help identify gaps in your program.

A downside to performing a first-party assessment is that it may not be as acceptable as a third-party assessment. This is because a first-party assessment is performed by you or your organization. This can oftentimes lead to higher scores or security controls that may have been overlooked. You may also score yourself more favorably than others because it is your program. It is also difficult to determine whether bias was used when answering questions. This is why third-party assessments are often acceptable to your customers and vendors rather than first-party assessments.

When performing a first-party assessment, be sure to leave your bias out of the equation. Bias can creep in by scoring yourself and the program higher than you should have on a particular control. Be sure to take a non-biased approach when answering the questions or scoring yourself on a particular control as this can provide a false sense of security.

Get familiar with the cybersecurity framework you intend to use for the assessment as well. This will help when asking questions regarding the control objectives used in the framework. You will need to ask the questions in such a way that it makes sense to everyone at the table as well. This is to make it easier for everyone to understand the objective of what is being asked.

If you intend to use the NIST CSF as the framework for your assessment, familiarize yourself with the controls and how you intend to use them. Come up with various ways of asking questions regarding the framework itself. Remember, you are oftentimes looking to ask questions that are not necessarily open-ended, but more than just a simple *yes* or *no*.

If you are new to the organization, I would highly recommend doing a first-party assessment anyway. It is a great way to get to know the people you are working with, and also get to know the technology and security stacks that are being used. Without doing this, how will you know what your future state will look like if you do not know where you are starting from?

Remember, the framework includes technical, physical, and administrative controls. You will need to write up everything that you do daily; this includes policies, standards, and procedures. You will need this information when training new employees along with supplying answers to auditors. Do yourself a favor and do not overlook or downplay this step.

Addressing the policies, standards, and procedures that are local to your department is a great first step in elevating your scores. Going from Tier 2 to Tier 3 will require that these policy documents now become organization-wide. This will require a program to be developed to sustain the level of maturity needed to continue to work through the policies.

Second-party assessments

Second-party assessments are performed by your customers or suppliers. A second-party assessment is meant to help you understand the security posture of an organization that currently does business with you and your organization. They also have a vested interest in ensuring that your organization is protecting sensitive information. For example, you may have customers who store sensitive information within your organization, and they want to ensure that your cybersecurity program is protecting their information to the best of your ability.

To better understand your cybersecurity culture, they will typically send out a questionnaire for you to fill out. This questionnaire can have several topics that pertain to data governance, policies and procedures, data protection, and cybersecurity best practices. You may also have findings from these questions that you must provide a response to. For example, you may be requested to change your incident response policy or include notifications to the customer in the event that an incident has occurred that has affected their information.

You may also intend to audit a supplier that you do business with to ensure that they are meeting the required SLAs. These typically include whether or not you are meeting the requirements, such as traceability, uptime, or how clean an environment is. This can often lead to contract disputes if an SLA is not met. Review your contracts to ensure that you are meeting their requirements.

I know of several large organizations that will fly their employees out on-site to conduct an assessment. This is to not only ensure that what they put down on paper is correct, but also to physically see the controls that were implemented. This will either help back up their claim of cybersecurity or show their flaws.

Third-party assessments

A **third-party assessment** is performed by an external party. This is often performed by an auditing firm or managed security services provider. While a third-party assessment is the preferred method, it is also the most expensive. This usually requires a team of people with varying specialties to come together and perform the assessment for you.

This is often the preferred method of performing the assessment as it takes the bias out completely from the scoring you do once the assessment has been completed. It is also the most widely accepted because of this. Customers and vendors may not accept a first-party assessment because of that bias.

A third-party assessment firm may or may not have the right staff to perform a review based on your given framework either. Work with the vendor to determine whether you can even perform the assessment based on the framework that you intend to use. While the Big 4 auditing firms may be able to perform an assessment based on the NIST CSF, smaller firms may not be able to due to a lack of expertise. Ensure that you are working with the correct vendor that will perform the assessment to your requirements.

Third-party assessors will typically provide a report on compliance with the framework, or at least provide you with a slide deck with their scores and findings. Other frameworks, such as ISO 27001, once passed all requirements, will provide you with a certification. This can be used to share with vendors and customers. However, you should have an NDA in place prior to providing this type of information to anyone.

Some regulatory requirements may request that you have a third-party assessment performed. This is where you will need to work with a compliance firm to perform the assessment on your behalf. Examples of this include some levels of PCI DSS, FedRAMP, GDPR, and CMMC.

The third-party assessor will ask for several items, including policies, standards, procedures, architectural diagrams, and configurations of systems. The auditor may also want to assess your logs and analyze your firewall rules to ensure that they meet your standards.

They may want to run scans across your network; this will also include your systems and services. These will involve scanning for configurations, vulnerabilities, and if there is any drift in your baseline. This will ensure that you are maintaining a standardized configuration throughout your environment.

Lastly, scope the assessment appropriately. If the scope of the assessment is only IT, keep it within IT. If it's for PCI, ensure that it stays within the cardholder data environment. Ensure that there are firewalls between the scoped environment and the rest of the network too. This will help keep you within scope and also keep your costs down as they are not assessing the entire environment.

Now, if you decide to perform the assessment yourself, there are several things you must consider. These include the following:

- The engagement letter
- Project kick-off

- Performing the assessment
- Performing the gap analysis
- Closeout

In the next section, we will discuss how to perform the assessment on your own.

Performing a self-assessment

When performing a self-assessment, or first-party assessment, there are several things you must have in place. These are all necessary to not only let everyone else know that you are performing the assessment but also act as a *get-out-of-jail-free* card. Let's take a look at what a first-party assessment entails.

The engagement letter

You will need to get approval from the CEO or someone in authority to allow you to perform the assessment. The engagement letter is meant to provide you with the authority to perform the assessment as you see fit. You may find that you need to perform certain types of security checks or scans across IT systems and services and it could potentially bring a system down. This all needs to be spelled out in the engagement letter.

The **engagement letter** should specifically state your intentions for the assessment and what you plan to get out of it. If you plan to use technology-based scanners to determine the configurations of systems and services and perform the assessment through question and answer sessions, and also need to have **subject matter experts (SMEs)** at the table, then this all needs to be spelled out in the letter itself.

The engagement letter should also have a schedule. This schedule is meant to provide guidance as to what you intend to do and when you intend to do it. For example, you may intend to interview all SMEs at the beginning of the week while by the end of the week, you may decide that you want to perform your scans. Or, maybe you want to review any previous assessments that were performed along with looking at architectural drawings and currently approved policies and procedures. This should all be laid out in your engagement letter.

Project kick-off

The **project kick-off** is when you start the assessment process. This is where you start the questionnaire by asking SMEs how they perform their job functions in relation to the framework. You will want to record their answers in a document for later review.

Again, the SMEs will not be as experienced in the framework as you are so ensure that you ask the questions in a certain way that your audience can understand. This can mean that you may have to expand on your questions to include examples or scenarios that will assist the SME in answering the question fully. Do not direct the SME in answering the question in a certain way, however; this can lead to bias in their answer as well.

Perform the assessment

This phase is when you are actually performing the assessment. You are asking questions of the SMEs and performing scans against IT resources. Remember to continue to use your engagement letter as a guide or outline for the process. This document spells out everything that you and the executive leadership team agreed to.

Avoid single-response questions, such as, "*Are backups performed?*" While this may be the root of the question, it does not allow for the SME to expand on the answer. Ask more open-ended questions, such as, "*How are backups performed?*" This not only allows for more than just a yes or no answer, but it also allows the SME to discuss the methodology of the backup process.

Listen to those in the room as well as the SME as they may have additional informationand pay special attention to non-verbal cues. This can help answer the questions or provide clarity about a particular process. It can also highlight where additional assistance may be needed for a particular function to work properly.

This is also the time when you should run your scans. These scans are meant to provide information as to how an IT resource was configured. You can use tools such as a vulnerability scanner or scan a service using the Center for Internet Security CIS-CAT. There are also other free scanners out there that you can use such as the DISA STIGs. These are meant to look at the configuration of a system or service and provide insight into your threat landscape.

You can also perform other types of scans, such as **open source intelligence** (**OSINT**), or look at DNS configurations. Both of these types of scans provide valuable information as to the types of services being used by the organization. These scans can also highlight sensitive files or information that should not be accessed by those on the internet. Discovering this type of information can help pinpoint where you may have data leakage or a misconfigured setting on a server.

If you have not already done so, this is also the time to review vulnerability scans, penetration test results, and architectural drawings, as well as policies, standards, and procedures. Performing an assessment such as this brings to light more than just how a system is configured, or whether or not you are performing backups; it is meant to review all documentation with regard to the environment under scope for the assessment.

Perform the gap analysis

By the end of the assessment, you should have all of your questions answered and all documentation reviewed. It is now time to wrap up the assessment and perform the gap analysis. The **gap analysis** is used to determine what is going on within the environment and where there needs to be improvement.

This is a critical step in the process as it will highlight where your deficiencies are so that you can develop project plans for how you want to tackle what is outstanding. This is also considered your current state; more on this later. What you will want to do, however, is rank your findings from most to least critical and begin to develop a game plan for how you intend to work on these findings.

Closeout

The **closeout** or exit interview is where you discuss your findings and report to the executive leadership team. The exit interview is used as a way of highlighting the organization's achievements and what they are doing right, as well as discussing the next steps.

You may also break up your findings into multiple different categories. For example, if you planned to perform the assessment based on the NIST CSF, you could break the scoring down by function or category. This scoring will help you identify where you need assistance in a particular area. An example of the scoring is as follows:

Continuous Monitoring (DE.CM)	
Subcategory	Score
DE.CM-01	25
DE.CM-02	75
DE.CM-03	50
DE.CM-06	50
DE.CM-09	25
Average Score	45

Table 11.1 – DE.CM average score

Now that we have a preliminary score for our current state, we can see how we align with the NIST CSF Tiers. Remember, the Tiers are based on a risk score and not a maturity index. If we want to see how the category aligns with the Tiering structure, we can quickly do so by assigning a scoring level to each tier. For example:

Tier	Score
Tier 1	25
Tier 2	50
Tier 3	75
Tier 4	100

Table 11.2 – Framework Tier scoring structure

As we can see, our DE.CM score falls within Tier 1, which is Risk Informed. This ultimately could mean that you have quite a few policies that are approved by management, but not organizational-wide. This scoring model will help you when determining where to focus your efforts on the overall NIST CSF.

When disclosing your results, be sure to rank them in order of importance. Develop project plans for how you intend to close the gaps for the various projects that may need to be spun up in order to mitigate the findings. Also, ask the business what is of most importance to them. There may be business cases for tackling a certain finding first.

Do this for all of the categories and generate the scores. This will provide you with an overall rating of the framework. This score will become important as we capture the current state and look toward creating our strategy.

Capturing the current state

Now that we have performed our assessment, it is time to determine our current state. Your current state is a culmination of the overall scores that were generated by the assessment, and any deficiencies that were discovered when reviewing any of the documentation.

As depicted in *Table 11.1*, we should have scores for all of the categories and subcategories that we based our assessment on. These scores include not only the technical controls but also the administrative controls. Technical controls are what we most likely think of when we think of a control. These are the firewalls, routers, servers, and any other physical equipment that we think of.

Administrative controls are those that we tend to not think of. These are the policies that need to be written to back up what we are doing for technical controls. We also need to include architectural drawings in addition to other documentation about the IT resource or process we are trying to implement.

All of this information can be tracked in a spreadsheet or database. This is to ensure that you are tracking the information appropriately. Also, ensure that your tracking mechanism also includes your future state.

Be sure to work with your executive leadership team while you are developing your current state. Use this time to better understand what their goals and objectives are from the assessment. This will come in handy for several reasons but mostly so you know what to prioritize when you are evaluating the results from the findings.

Rank your results based on the level of risk your organization is willing to take. You may show that you ranked really well in the Detect function but seem to be lacking considerably with Response and Recover. If your organization needs to refocus its efforts on incident response, this would be the time to change direction. These are the conversations that you need to have with senior leadership.

Creating your future roadmap

Now that we have gone through the analysis of our current state and scored ourselves based on the scoring model found in *Table 11.2*, we should now begin to determine our future state. The future state is where we plan to be in the next three to five years. Not only will we need to take a risk-based approach to how we develop our strategies, but we also need to ensure that the goals we put forward are attainable.

First and foremost, you need to look at how you can reduce the largest amount of risk with the least amount of effort. It is not because you are lazy; rather, it is because you are trying to reduce the biggest amount of risk possible with the least amount of resources. This could be introducing a new password standard, writing new policies, or developing architectural drawings.

The longer-termed projects, such as introducing **multifactor authentication** (**MFA**), integrating all applications with single sign-on, or introducing a new logging standard, can still be planned, however, they will take time to implement. Work with your various teams to ensure that you will have resources allocated to the projects. These projects will also help reduce the amount of organizational risk your company has.

We again also need to take into account our conversations with the executive leadership team and board of directors. Each of these groups will set the tone for what you need to achieve and by when. If you are tasked with getting your incident response and detection processes put together, then this will be part of your strategy moving forward when aligning with the Response and Recover functions of the framework.

SMART goals

Put together goals for both tactical and strategic projects. This will help with assigning resources and deadlines for the initiative. There are several different ways of going about how to do this. **SMART goals** are typically what is used for this:

- **Specific**: This is the exact goal you are trying to achieve. Whether it is implementing new firewall rules, or installing a Linux web server, this is the thing that you are working toward.

- **Measurable**: How can you determine the success or failure of a project? This involves building in metrics or numbers to better understand how you are achieving your goals.

- **Achievable**: Is your goal obtainable? Can you obtain your specific goal within the measured amount of time?

- **Relevant**: Does the goal align with your business objectives? This is where input from your executive leadership teams will be needed. Without the backing from them, your projects or initiatives may go nowhere.

- **Time-bound**: The goal or objective needs to have a deadline. Without this, it is very difficult to measure progress when you have no deadline to meet.

A SMART goal could be as follows:

- **Specific**: Develop an approach of implementing an incident response program

- **Measurable**: Obtain at least a 3.0 on the scoring model

- **Achievable**: Set touchpoints every six months to re-evaluate our scores to determine progress

- **Relevant**: The executive leadership team has expressed an increased concern about a ransomware event occurring
- **Time-bound**: Obtain the 3.0 score for the Recover and Response functions within the next 18 months

Future state scoring model

Similar to how we scored ourselves in *Table 11.1*, we should now have our scores for the rest of the categories. This makes up our current state. We now need to evaluate ourselves and our resources and align our objectives to the SMART goals we created. This will allow us to develop the future state score. This future state is what our strategic roadmap will consist of.

If you are first starting out, you may have no foundation and will need to build it from the ground up. When doing this, it is important to remember that you need to not only introduce new technical controls but also work on your administrative ones. This will consist of a lot of new technologies and documentation.

Incident Management (RS.MA)		
Subcategory	**Current State**	**Future State**
RS.MA-01	25	50
RS.MA-02	50	75
RS.MA-03	50	75
RS.MA-04	25	75
RS.MA-05	25	50
Average Score	35	65

Table 11.3 – Incident management scores

Do this for the rest of the functions found in the framework to provide yourself with a score that you aim to achieve. Again, work with your executive team as well when creating the future state scores. They may want you to align more with their objectives for the business and the direction the executive team will want to take.

Look at the latest trends and understand threats and risks as well. Over the past several years, there has been an increased focus on supply chain risk management and social engineering. While you may want to focus on the exciting aspects of cybersecurity that you get from detection and response, you may want to focus on identity management.

There are several projects that you should spin up if you have not done so already. This includes the creation of an enterprise risk management dashboard. You can break out local risk management dashboards, which could be project-specific. As you begin to identify risks associated with an environment, keep track of those risks and develop a **Plan of Action and Milestones (POA&M)** to remediate the deficiencies.

As you continue to build out those localized risk dashboards, float the higher or risky ones up to an enterprise dashboard. This dashboard will have oversight of the risks that should be reviewed on a monthly basis. As you close out those risks, mark them closed; never delete them.

This will allow you to provide a historical view of the process and projects used to close out the identified risk. You will want to keep this information for audit purposes. Having a good risk identification process will also help you with transparency. Remember, you cannot drive zero risk – it is not possible. However, you have to take care of risks that make sense in protecting your organization.

Another good strategy to work on is **identity and access management (IAM)**. Promoting the use of single sign-on and enforcing MFA everywhere. You will need to have good policies and procedures in place to get everyone involved on the same page when it comes to security. Take quick action if and when you know of someone's account being compromised.

Back up your IAM strategy with a solid understanding of password management as well. Work with vendors of your IAM application to enforce the use of the following:

- Reduce or eliminate the number of common passwords
- Do not allow the use of a username in the password
- Educate users on the dangers of using pets' or children's names

Promote the use of passkeys to authenticate to IT resources. Passkeys are a new way of authenticating to given IT resources. Passkeys were developed as a more secure way of accessing systems through the FIDO2 protocol. It essentially creates a public/private key pair used for authentication.

The biggest advantage of using a passkey instead of a password is that each passkey is unique to the resource. This prevents the use of password duplication across multiple accounts. It also prevents account takeovers as, again, the public key of the passkey must be registered with the authentication service. If you are duped into going to a lookalike phishing page requesting credentials, you cannot provide them because you registered with a passkey and not a password.

Summary

In this last chapter, we discussed how to perform an assessment, along with developing the current and future state roadmaps. These roadmaps are used to understand your current environment and also to develop a strategic plan of where you want your security program to go in the next three to five years.

There are pros and cons to how one should conduct the assessment. If you decide that you want to perform an assessment on your own, this is called a first-party assessment. This is the least expensive, albeit, fun approach to understanding your environment.

Pay attention to the documents that need to be created first. You will need to have an engagement letter stating that you are allowed to perform the assessment. This should spell out your intentions for the assessment and how you intend to conduct it. If you decide that you are going to perform configuration scans, ensure that is also in the letter.

Once the assessment is complete, score yourself against the tiering risk model discussed earlier in this book. This will provide you with an understanding of your current posture. You should collect all of the deficiencies that came out of the assessment as we will turn these into future projects.

These projects will turn into your future state or what you want to achieve. When calculating your current state, calculate your future state scores as well. This will provide you with where you are aiming to be. Develop SMART goals as well to ensure that you are staying on target and the goals are meaningful.

There may be some projects that do not require excessive resources and can greatly reduce the amount of risk your organization faces. Work with your executive team and board of directors to provide guidance on what projects they think should be included in the remediation list as well. Ensure that you align your strategic future goals with business objectives.

Lastly, I would like to thank all of you for picking up and reading this book. I hope you found the book's contents insightful and helpful on your journey toward alignment with the NIST Cybersecurity Framework. If you are new to cybersecurity or have found yourself leading a team of cybersecurity professionals, you may want to get my first book, *Executive's Cybersecurity Program Handbook*. This book is meant for newly hired heads of cybersecurity or CISOs who have never had an opportunity to develop a program from the ground up.

If you have any questions, please feel free to reach out:

`https://jasonbrown.us`

`jason@jasonbrown.us`

Index

packtpub.com

Subscribe to our online digital library for full access to over 7,000 books and videos, as well as industry leading tools to help you plan your personal development and advance your career. For more information, please visit our website.

Why subscribe?

- Spend less time learning and more time coding with practical eBooks and Videos from over 4,000 industry professionals

- Improve your learning with Skill Plans built especially for you

- Get a free eBook or video every month

- Fully searchable for easy access to vital information

- Copy and paste, print, and bookmark content

Did you know that Packt offers eBook versions of every book published, with PDF and ePub files available? You can upgrade to the eBook version at packtpub.com and as a print book customer, you are entitled to a discount on the eBook copy. Get in touch with us at customercare@packtpub.com for more details.

At www.packtpub.com, you can also read a collection of free technical articles, sign up for a range of free newsletters, and receive exclusive discounts and offers on Packt books and eBooks.

Other Books You May Enjoy

If you enjoyed this book, you may be interested in these other books by Packt:

Introduction to Kali Purple

Karl Lane

ISBN: 978-1-83508-898-2

- Set up and configure a fully functional miniature security operations center

- Explore and implement the government-created Malcolm suite of tools

- Understand traffic and log analysis using Arkime and CyberChef

- Compare and contrast intrusion detection and prevention systems

- Explore incident response methods through Cortex, TheHive, and threat intelligence feed integration

- Leverage purple team techniques for social engineering and exploit development

Unveiling the NIST Risk Management Framework (RMF)

Thomas Marsland

ISBN: 978-1-83508-984-2

- Understand how to tailor the NIST Risk Management Framework to your organization's needs
- Come to grips with security controls and assessment procedures to maintain a robust security posture
- Explore cloud security with real-world examples to enhance detection and response capabilities
- Master compliance requirements and best practices with relevant regulations and industry standards
- Explore risk management strategies to prioritize security investments and resource allocation
- Develop robust incident response plans and analyze security incidents efficiently

Packt is searching for authors like you

If you're interested in becoming an author for Packt, please visit `authors.packtpub.com` and apply today. We have worked with thousands of developers and tech professionals, just like you, to help them share their insight with the global tech community. You can make a general application, apply for a specific hot topic that we are recruiting an author for, or submit your own idea.

Share Your Thoughts

Now you've finished *Unveiling NIST Cybersecurity Framework 2.0*, we'd love to hear your thoughts! Scan the QR code below to go straight to the Amazon review page for this book and share your feedback or leave a review on the site that you purchased it from.

`https://packt.link/r/183546307X`

Your review is important to us and the tech community and will help us make sure we're delivering excellent quality content.

Download a free PDF copy of this book

Thanks for purchasing this book!

Do you like to read on the go but are unable to carry your print books everywhere?

Is your eBook purchase not compatible with the device of your choice?

Don't worry, now with every Packt book you get a DRM-free PDF version of that book at no cost.

Read anywhere, any place, on any device. Search, copy, and paste code from your favorite technical books directly into your application.

The perks don't stop there, you can get exclusive access to discounts, newsletters, and great free content in your inbox daily

Follow these simple steps to get the benefits:

1. Scan the QR code or visit the link below

https://packt.link/free-ebook/978-1-83546-307-9

2. Submit your proof of purchase
3. That's it! We'll send your free PDF and other benefits to your email directly

www.ingramcontent.com/pod-product-compliance
Lightning Source LLC
Chambersburg PA
CBHW080530060326

40690CB00022B/5083